THE UNIVERSITY OF LIFE

Mehdi N. Bahadori, Ph D

Published by Blue Dolphin Publishing, Inc.
P.O. Box 1920, Nevada City, CA 95959
Orders: 1 (800) 643-0765

Library of Congress Cataloging-in-Publication Data
    The university of life / Mehdi N. Bahadori.
        p.   cm.
      ISBN 0-931892-70-8 : $7.95
      1. Spiritual life. 2. Spiritual formation. 3. Life.
      I. Title
    BV4501.2.B27 1993
    291.4'4—dc20   93-41303
                                                  CIP

  ISBN 0-931892-70-8 $7.95

Printed in the United States of America

It is to the students, teachers, and the supporting staff of

THE UNIVERSITY OF LIFE

that this book is dedicated.

PREFACE

Several months ago I wrote a short article called "this University," and presented it at one of the monthly workshops of the Omega Vector Organization in Phoenix. On occasion I shared the article with several friends. Later, I sent it for publication in the Venture Inward Magazine.

Subsequently, I wrote a few other short articles (not yet published), sharing them with friends. They made suggestions and comments, thereby encouraging me to expand the articles. This little book is the result.

Many people commented on the manuscript. I am grateful to all of them. I would specifically like to acknowledge Carol McNally and Louisa von Dessau for their comments; Lesley Vann for editing the final version of the manuscript and Paul Balyoz for typing it. I asked Ana Mayse to read the completed manuscript, developing illustrations for each chapter. She was able to capture in a marvelous way the message of each chapter. I am grateful to her for all these illustrations, and for illustrating the cover.

I invite you to really look at these illustrations before and after reading each chapter. See if the messages you get are the same. Please observe the cover once again, upon finishing the book. See what message it conveys to you then! For me, the cover has a special spiritual significance.

Mehdi N. Bahadori
Tempe, Arizona
July, 1987

TABLE OF CONTENTS

ii

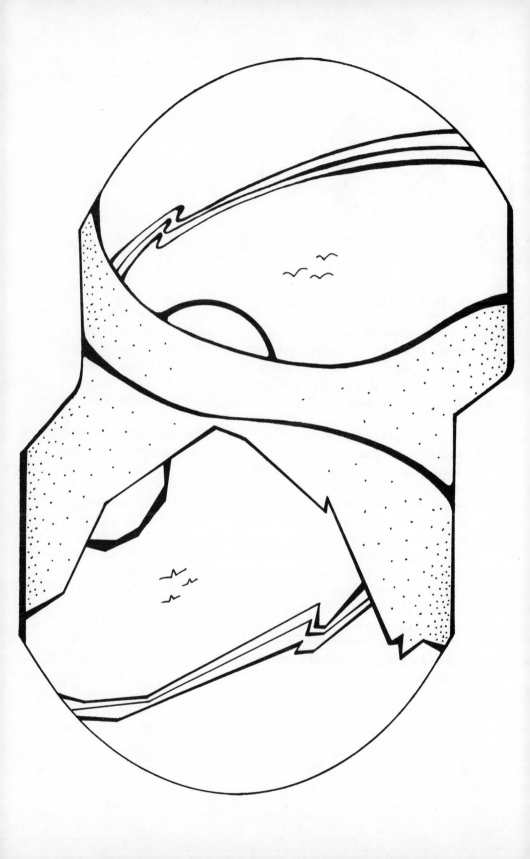

1. INTRODUCTION

How often do we hear the expression: "why did it happen to me?"

In our daily life we see some people who have a hard time making a living, or making ends meet. Everything is going wrong for them and they do not seem to have any control over their lives. On the other hand, we know of other people who do not seem to make much effort but have a wonderful time, and everything seems to fall in place for them perfectly.

If you have seen an assembly-line production of automobiles or other industrial or agricultural products, you know what I mean when I say everything falls in at the right time and place for people without any extraordinary effort on their part. If you watch an assembly line, for example in an automobile manufacturing plant, you see that parts are coming from various directions, work is done on some, partial assembly is done on several other parts, they are then placed on another line, and so on. Finally, all the lines converge at a point where final assembly is carried out. You do not see anybody running around fetching parts, or making an extraordinary effort. The person stationed at a given location has faith in the system. He knows that the parts he needs to work on will be there when he needs them. He does not have to worry about anything; he knows that everything has been accounted for and is taken care of. He knows that everything is going smoothly, and cars will be produced at a predetermined rate.

1

If it were not for such a smooth and effortless operation (in manufacturing of automobiles, and other industrial and agricultural products), man
could not have all the conveniences of life that he is enjoying now.

The opposite to this is also true. Imagine going to an auto repair shop
to have your car fixed, where the mechanic does not seem to find what he is
looking for. He has to go to different places to find every tool that he
needs, or yell to his assistants to help him locate it. This is complete
chaos. You get tired watching the man work, and most probably he does
not enjoy working this way, either. He definitely does not make as much
money as he would if he were more organized.

People experience these two extreme ways of life, as well as everything
in between. There are times when nothing seems to be going right for a
family; when everything falls apart and the people have a miserable time;
and times when people live their lives in total peace and harmony, with very
little effort to get things done.

Let me expand a little more on this paradox, and the diversity of human
experience. We often wonder about the inequities of life. We see, for
example, that babies are born to kings, queens, political leaders, and wealthy
families with a secure material future, where they do not have to worry
about anything. We also see that at the same time in the same city other
babies are born handicapped, unwanted, to be abused by their parents, and
with not much of a future. Between these two extremes, there are thousands
of babies born every day throughout the world, each one with a unique
background and each one needing to cope, in his or her* own way, with the
innate problems of living on this planet. Each one is struggling to make it
on this planet, and each one is carving a different future for himself.

We often wonder if there is any justice behind all of this. Here we see
one child who will have every convenience life has to offer, and another who

---

*To be fair to both male and female readers, I should be using both masculine
and feminine pronouns. In order to conserve space, however, the traditional
usage of the masculine pronoun referring to *both* genders will be used
throughout this book.

does not seem to have anything, and will have to struggle everyday to live. What is the point behind all this? Whose fault is it, the baby's or the parents', if a baby is born handicapped, unwanted, and to be abused throughout his life? Or is it anybody's fault at all? Is it possible that behind all these extreme living conditions and all the ones in between, there are some *lessons* to be learned? If there are lessons, what are they, who decides them, and when?

In this book I would like to present a concept, or a hypothesis, which I believe will answer the above questions: That there is, indeed, justice in Creation, and everything is happening for a reason and for the good of man. It is up to us to find out what it is!

The Method for Presenting the Concept

This book is divided into several short chapters. In chapter two, I will present several cases: real stories of people who have had hard times in life. Chapter three deals with the usefulness of developing a life philosophy or hypothesis in order to understand life and events better. Developing hypotheses is common in both the physical and behavioral sciences. It seems acceptable that I, too, can develop a hypothesis in order to answer many questions about life on this planet.

In chapter four the concept of *The University of Life* will be presented, where one may look at events not as accidents or the faults or mistakes of one person or a few people. We will consider the possibility that it is the choice of each individual before birth to carve his or her own destiny; that each on of us is just a student in this University (or the University of Life): learning our lessons and moving up to a higher grade, *that every event is nothing but a lesson.*

In chapter five a brief mention is made of what the lessons are for us to learn. Chapter six looks at the events of life in the light of the concept of the University of Life which is presented here, and in chapter seven a few tips are presented on how to study in this University.

In chapter eight I compare myself with what people commonly confuse me with. I consider my body as a study kit, and as a vehicle to take me around. In chapter nine, a comparison is made between the hardware and software of a microcomputer, and my body and soul.

Chapter ten deals with the journey of a water droplet as it moves through life, eventually reaching its beloved, and becoming one with the ocean. Chapter eleven points out that actually we have never been apart from God, or the University Master. Finally, chapter twelve asks the question: why is Creation the way it is, and why God has established the University of Life? No definite answer is given, and the reader is given the opportunity to consider this for himself.

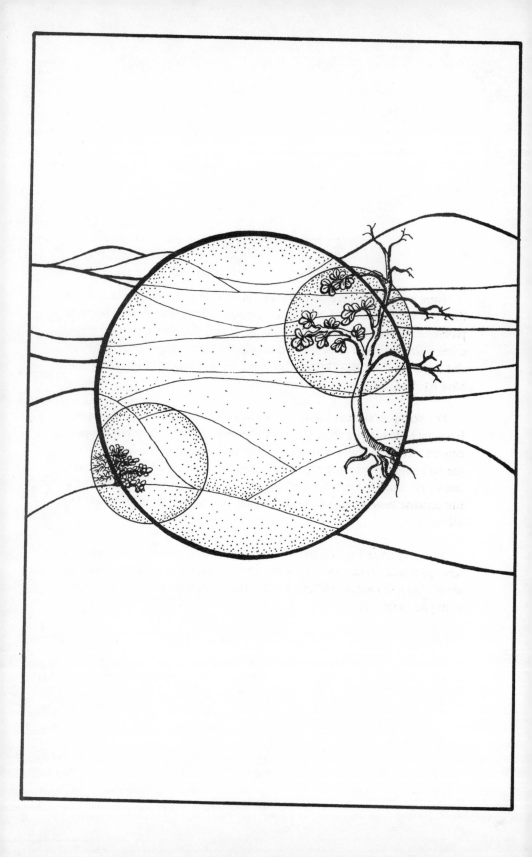

2. A FEW EXPERIENCES

There are many people we know who have had exceptional experiences in life, and have really had hard times living. They either overcame their problems, learned from their experiences, or they simply succumbed to the crisis. We often hear of people who could not cope with a certain problem and committed suicide. On the other hand, we also hear of other people who have handled really tough problems in life.

For example, we may know of a woman who, through a natural disaster, loses her husband, her children, and all her belongings, and becomes handicapped. Yet, she copes with the problem and builds her life anew. While she will never forget these experiences, she manages to find hope in her life, and carries on. On the other hand, we commonly find people who take their life because they are unable to accept that their spouse or beloved one has left them.

In this chapter I would like to consider a few of the examples which I have personally witnessed. They have helped me reach my understandings about life, and have helped me develop the hypothesis which I am sharing with you in this book.

My Father's and Uncle's Deaths

My father, who died four years ago, was bed ridden for nearly ten years. For a man who could not sit still and had to always be outside and on the move, this was a big disappointment. He really suffered in being confined to a small room. He had a hard and difficult life, and did a lot of things in his early years. My uncle, on the other hand, died of a heart attack on the street while shopping. He apparently did not suffer at all, as he died shortly after the attack. Here are two brothers, about two years apart, both having somewhat similar lifestyles, but one dying with a great deal of pain, and the other apparently with none.

Baby Maryam Going Blind

In 1968 I was teaching at Shiraz University (then called Pahlavi University) in Iran. A colleague of mine, Dr. Ali —, received a telephone call from his wife that Maryam, their six-month-old baby daughter had gone blind and could not see a thing. He rushed home and found that indeed the baby did not visually respond to any movements or objects near her eyes. She was fine the night before, and the mother discovered her condition when she awoke that morning. The parents were horrified with the incident and rushed the baby to Khalili Hospital. This hospital was well known throughout the Middle East for its modern facilities and good doctors. After several days of examinations, the doctors told them that they could not find the problem, as they had never seen or read anything like it before. They then suggested that the parents may want to take the baby to Tehran, and have her eyes examined by several other doctors and specialists.

This was a shock and great sorrow for all of us in the community. We all expressed our feelings to Ali and his wife, and prayed for the baby's rapid recovery. Ali, being totally heart-broken, took the rest of the semester off, and together with his wife, took Maryam to Tehran. The doctors in Tehran, after days of examinations, could not find what was wrong with the baby either. They suggested the baby be taken to Europe or America, where certain doctors they knew could possibly help.

Money was not a major problem for Ali, as he was a wealthy man and could afford the high costs of travel to Europe and the United States, and could also afford to pay all the specialists to examine and treat Maryam's eyes. They made arrangements with their parents to come to Shiraz and take care of their other daughter.

They left Tehran for Austria, where several physicians had been recommended to see the baby. After a few weeks in Vienna and in-depth examinations by several doctors, the diagnosis was the same: the cause of the blindness was unknown, and so was its treatment.

The doctors, in turn, recommended other specialists in other European cities. The same thing happened with these doctors. They, in turn, recommended others. After spending a few months in Europe the parents finally came to the States to see a doctor who was highly recommended by all others. He was a Professor at Johns Hopkins University in Maryland. He was the last hope for the heart-broken parents.

After several days of testing, the Professor told them frankly that he did not know what the problem was, and therefore could not prescribe any solution. He told them that, instead of staying in Baltimore and paying a lot of money for further testing, they should return home and hope for a miracle. He said that he did not know of anyone who could possibly help the baby.

After four months and several thousand dollars of expenses, the heart-broken parents returned to Shiraz. I saw them at their home, tired and in total grief. They did not know what had gone wrong, and certainly did not know what they should do next. Ali could not concentrate on his teaching any longer and resigned his position at the University. A few months later the whole family moved to Tehran. Before they left Shiraz, however, the miracle indeed happened.

Revelations Came Through I knew a man of God in Shiraz by the name of Haji Kamal. He was a poet, a Sufi, and a teacher of Persian literature in high schools. (Although he had a law degree from the University of Tehran, he chose not to practice law. He thought he could reach people better by teaching.)

Haji Kamal had the ability to contact advanced souls through a technique not unlike hypnosis. He used to hold sessions at his house twice a week, where many people (mostly his former students) would come to listen to him talk about God, reading Persian poetry by Rumi, Hafez, Sa'di and other poets, including himself. Once in a while he would also contact an advanced soul for the solution to a problem, or for spiritual guidance. It was from Haji Kamal I learned the concept of Unity of God: that *there is only one being in the world, and it is God.* Everything and everybody is a manifestation, or a face of God.

With my knowledge of Haji Kamal's background and ability, and the grief of my friend and his family about their daughter's condition, I decided to invite them all for a gathering at my place to see what would happen. Haji Kamal had a general response to almost any question: "whatever God wants will happen."

At my home after a short conversation with our guests, Haji Kamal randomly opened the poetry book of Hafez. He asked a fellow with a good voice to recite the poem with a melody. It was amazing how relevant this was for the occasion. What it said, essentially, was, "I know you are heartbroken and have given up hope, *but things will work out and in God you will find hope.*"

Hafez's poetry is known throughout Iran as the source to answer your questions and grievances. Although his poems are open to interpretation, everyone seems to get results. You simply hold the book closed, and with your eyes also closed say a little prayer to him and mentally state your question. Then you just open the book to a page completely at random, not looking for any specific poem. Whichever poem you find contains the answer to your question.

Hafez's poem was so interesting and appropriate for the occasion that everybody present (aware of the baby's condition, and the family's grievances) cried. While all the doctors had given up hope, and the family had none left either, the group found a poem, written over six hundred years ago, which finally offered invaluable hope. A feeling of joy and expectation welled up among this circle of friends.

Through one of the people present, Haji Kamal then contacted an advanced soul in the spiritual realm. This was a man whom Haji Kamal had met several years before, when he was alive, and had high regard for him. When contacted, the higher soul, speaking through the medium, said that "the baby will be able to see in three weeks. The parents need not do anything, but if they so choose, they may give to charity and help the poor." This, confirming the poem of Hafez, brought more tears to the eyes of those present, and gave a lot of hope to the heart-broken parents. Haji Kamal now had no doubt that the baby would be able to see soon. He had great confidence in the predictions of this man of God and Hafez's poetry.

After this incident, Ali became very generous and gave a great deal to charities. One night I went with him to the poorer section of town, where he had loaded his Mercedes with food and distributed it door to door to the poor. I am sure it was the first time he had been to that part of town; it certainly was the first time for me to see all those people living in such poverty in an oil-rich country like Iran.

The Baby's Eyes Improved In exactly three weeks the baby's eyes started to respond to movements. She was able to see light after nearly six months of total darkness.

After a few weeks, the family moved to Tehran. When I visited them later that year, they were so happy with the change. They had become so loving and giving. They said that they had corresponded with the Professor at Johns Hopkins University, and had told him about what happened. The response from the Professor was: "It has been a miracle. I could not find out what caused the blindness and do not certainly know now what cured it. I am happy for the baby and all of you."

Akram Dying of Cancer

A distant relative of mine by the name of Akram, a lady in her thirties with two young children, had cancer and for two years suffered from the most excruciating pain. She was given all kinds of drugs by her doctors to relieve the pain, but none seemed to have any appreciable effect. Her relatives' and friends' prayers for her were not so much for her to get well, as they knew there was no cure for her cancer, but for her to die and not suffer so much.

Why do These Events Take Place?

I have observed these and many other incidents in the lives of my relatives, friends, and others. I have often wondered about the reason for these occurrences. These events have greatly influenced my thinking. I have often asked why things happen the way they do. Two brothers, one dying in difficulty and the other with total ease; a baby becoming blind, without apparent cause, then getting well, and her recovery being predicted by higher souls; and a young woman dying in such pain. What is going on here? What did God want to demonstrate in all these incidents?

There must be an explanation for all of these and other events that we witness everyday. I am sure that everyone can sit down and prepare a long list of all the relatives and friends who died at ease or in pain, had a good and easy life, or whose lives were in total disarray. We can list all these events and still wonder why things happen to these people. Why did such a kind and good family have to suffer so much? Why did people who were so generous with time and money have to suffer from natural disasters, accidents, crimes, and so on? Had they committed earlier sins for which they were now being punished? What are the reasons? Of course one needs to find the answer.

Through many years of observing these events, reading and learning about religious and spiritual teachings from all sources (particularly in the Persian literature and poetry), attending Haji Kamal's sessions, and finally attending seminars and lectures on various spiritual subjects, I have come to develop a hypothesis through which I can now satisfy my own curiosity, thus answering my own questions.

In this book I would like to share this hypothesis with you. In presenting this metaphorical perspective, I am not claiming to answer any religious or metaphysical question. I do not claim any authority on any of these subjects. I simply have an idea that I would like to share with you. My hope is that by accepting it, it will help you understand life more.

Further, my hope is that you will accept people as they are; not to be critical of them and not expect them to change and be the way you want them to be; that you may accept everyone as having a mission in life; and everyone as working through this in his "own sweet way," taking all the time he needs; that you may come to accept and love yourself just the same.

In this book I would like to present an explanation for all the above events. I do so by presenting a hypothesis which looks at *life on Earth as attendance in a university: THE UNIVERSITY OF LIFE.* Events and so-called "accidents" are then simply *lessons to be learned.* Everybody we meet is learning his lessons, and at the same time is playing the important role of teaching us something. It is only right to respect and honor our teachers. Furthermore, in the University of Life, things do not happen by accident; they are lessons for us and there are reasons for their occurrences.

3. THE USEFULNESS OF HYPOTHESES

In our life we often develop hypotheses or "models" to describe, understand, and see things better. In department stores we see mannequins or live
models displaying clothing, making it easier for the potential customer to
visualize how certain clothing will fit. In architecture we build models to
see the relationships between different sections of a building, and how it
will actually appear. In the physical sciences we also build models, mostly
mathematical, in order to describe and understand certain events better.

Religions have also created "models" such as heaven and hell, so their
followers will be able to picture what could happen to them if they do or do
not do certain things. I am not going to discuss the concept of hell and
heaven and what they are. I am no authority on religions. I just want to
point out that man often develops hypotheses and models to understand his
surroundings better.

The models used by the department stores for clothing and by the archi-
tects to display their building designs are but simple examples to prove my
point. Being familiar with the physical sciences and engineering, I can
think of numerous mathematical models used for this purpose. The laws of
mechanics, dealing with motion, and the laws of thermodynamics, dealing
with the conversion of energy, are examples where mathematical models are
employed to describe physical events. The scientists build these models to
describe how things happen. Once new knowledge is gained in an area
which does not agree with the existing model or hypothesis, or when new
questions are raised and the existing hypothesis cannot answer them, then

scientists modify their models so they can describe the events in light of new findings.

Building models is also common in behavioral sciences. Although not often exact and mathematical in nature, there exist models which describe human behavior. For example, psychologists often relate certain crimes to the upbringing of the individual. They would say, for example, that a child who has been abused is likely to become a child abuser when he grows up. They do not say that every child abuser today has been abused in the past, or every child being abused now will become one when he grows up. But they find that these events are related. Based on their findings, they may attach a percentage or probability to the above statement. There are also other models, although not as exact as in the physical sciences.

So, developing models to describe events is not anything new. Models have been used by man throughout history. We change our models in order to understand new phenomena. We develop entirely new theories, discarding the old ones which no longer serve our purposes.

Man once maintained that the Earth was flat. This opinion, or model, was based on his observations. He found that this model or belief was no longer valid when it could not answer his emerging questions. So he simply discarded it and developed a new one: that the Earth is round. With this new model he could answer many questions and satisfy his curiosity. It was indeed this concept which lead to the discovery of America. Columbus could not have supported the old concept of the Earth being flat, and still travel where he did to find what he discovered.

Developing models is one of our enjoyments in life. Look around and see how many opinionated people there are. Ask people a question about politics, health, the causes of crime, poverty, etc., and see how many different opinions are expressed. Each one has, in his own mind, a hypothesis or model to describe the events he witnesses everyday.

I am not different from any of these people, and have developed my own model or hypothesis which answers many questions I have had. I have raised some of these questions above.

I would like to emphasize that I do not expect you to accept my hypothesis. You may want to reject it altogether, accept part and reject the rest, or you may want to develop your own model. What I have wanted to do in this book is to share with you a hypothesis I have found which answers my questions about life.

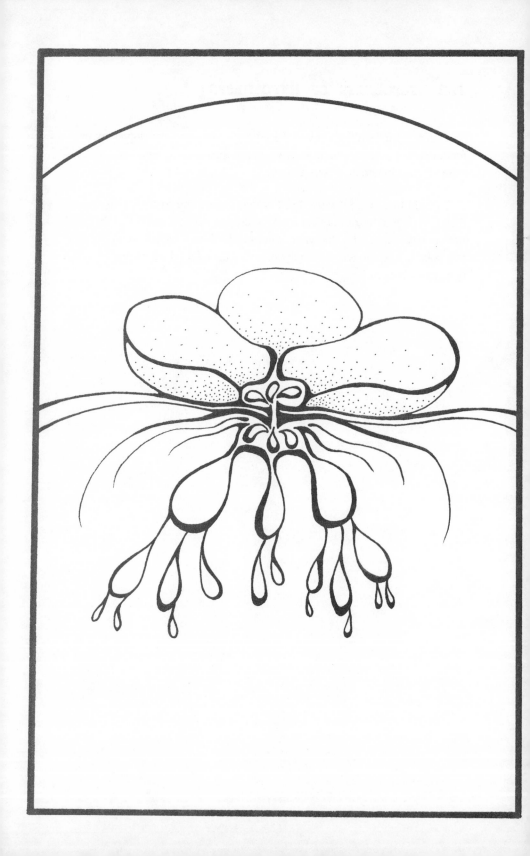

4. THE CONCEPT OF THE UNIVERSITY OF LIFE

Having spent a great portion of my life in educational institutions, both as a student and as a professor, it should not be surprising that I would relate the events I have witnessed, and my observations of the world around me, to education. Relating events to one's job or profession is common among many people. Listen to how different people describe their experiences in terms of their daily occupations. I am no exception.

Conventional Universities

First let us consider what a conventional university consists of. You may be quite familiar with the operation of universities. If so, you may want to skip this section. But before doing so, please go over the items highlighted here. I would like to draw a parallel between the concept of the University of Life and conventional universities. Therefore, I am describing the operation of both.

Although universities differ, I believe almost all of them have the following elements in common:

Campus A conventional university consists of one or more campuses. This is basically one or more large pieces of land set aside for the development of the university. It houses the class rooms, laboratories, faculty and staff offices, athletic and recreational facilities, and dormitories for the

17

students. In some instances, where a university is being developed in a small town with insufficient housing (particularly in developing countries where housing is always a problem), there may exist housing for faculty and staff as well.

Administration The administration generally consists of the university master, president, or chancellor, and several officers. The officers, appointed by the university president, are responsible for various functions of the university. The university president generally sets the short- and long-range policies, is responsible for day to day activities, and looks after the welfare of the students and faculty as a whole.

A good university president, as well as any of the officers of the university, is completely impartial toward the students' age, color, sex, proficiency, and lifestyle. For them, a student entering the university for the first time is the same as one returning from summer break, or one finishing a doctoral program. They know that freshmen students will someday graduate from the university, as others have done before them.

Faculty I like to think that the faculty of any university is its most important asset. It is the faculty which makes the university what it is. The rest exists so that the faculty can do its job, which is the educating and training of young minds. The faculty is that element of the university preparing the students to assume responsible positions in society, which in turn helps the progress and welfare of the people supporting the university.

The faculty on a campus can be identified generally by their age, and gray hair, or lack thereof. Exceptions can be found in this statement. There are many students who are older than their professors. When I was an assistant professor at the University of Missouri at Rolla, I taught a night course to practicing engineers where I was younger than most of the students in the class. But that was several years ago. There are no disguises, and it is not often difficult to discern the faculty or teachers from the students in conventional universities. This is not the case in the University of Life, as we shall soon see.

Except for the above distinctions, the faculty and students, in their interaction, learn from one another in classrooms and laboratories. Although the faculty may learn more than the students (and as such can be considered "students" themselves), these teachers nevertheless are paid for their function. The students, however, in almost all cases, must pay to attend the university.

Student Body The student body is the most important element of any university structure. It is because of the students that a university is established.

Supporting Staff These are the people who make the university function as it does. They are the secretaries, the personnel, the maintenance and the cleaning people, and all of those folks who provide a valuable service to the operation of the university, but are generally the lowest paid individuals on campus.

Program of Study and Lessons To do an effective job in teaching young minds, one needs to devise a program of study for each student. Each program of study generally consists of several theoretical or experimental lessons, lectures, field trips, etc. These provide the incentives for the students to attend the university in the first place. Although one may find a few students who go to a university for social and other reasons, they are more the exception than the rule.

Admission Policies To enter a university one has to have a certain background or education. Not anyone can be admitted to the conventional universities. This discrimination is needed because there are often more applicants than there is room for in a university. The university administration has to set policies (for the staff to follow) to only admit certain types of students. There were times (and still there are places in the world) when the students were discriminated against because of color or sex. But the number of these universities is decreasing. Now most of the admission policies are based on the scholastic background of the applicants.

Examinations and Probationary Policies The students' perform-
ances are often evaluated by the professors in the form of grades. When a
student has not performed satisfactorily, he is first placed on probation, and
if he does not perform well during this period, he is asked to leave the
university.

Academic Year and the Summer Vacation The students do not
normally attend the university continuously. The university administration
knows that the students need time to rest, reflect, and get away from all the
hassles of campus life, and make decisions about their future. For this
reason they have divided the calendar year into an academic year with a summer vacation.

Why summer has been chosen as the vacation time is not a major issue
for us here. (Perhaps it was originally felt that the students could help their
parents on the farm during this season.) The important point is that there
exists a period in the university calendar when the students may be absent
for whatever reason. Of course, the universities do not shut down during
this period. There may be students who want to take special courses during
summer, finish their research, or whatever.

Scholarship While students usually pay part of their educational expenses, the university may offer financial assistance to some. Scholastical-
ly better students may receive financial help, in the form of scholarships, to
assist their professors in their teaching or research, to tutor weaker students
or lower classmen, conduct laboratory courses, accompany students on field
trips, etc. Other students may receive help in assisting the supporting staff
of the university.

Although not very common, a university may also give free room and
board to all or some of their students and then ask them to do extra chores
such as working in the kitchen or the dormitories, or things of that nature.

Degrees Offered After the students finish their studies, that is, when
they have fulfilled all the requirements of a program of study, they are then
offered a diploma to certify that they have earned a degree. There are basic-

ally several degrees that the students in a conventional university seek: Bachelor of Science (or Art), Master of Science (or Art, or Education), Doctorate of Philosophy (or Education, or Engineering), and so on. There are many areas and fields of study.

Special Teaching or Research Appointments After a student has earned the highest degree, which is usually a doctorate, he no longer needs to enroll at the university as a student. Depending on the special needs of the university, however, some of the graduates or alumni who have been exceptionally successful in their career may be invited to come back to the university on special appointments. These appointments could be, for example, to give special instructions, interact with gifted students, or help the ones who may have difficulty in their studies. These alumni are at the university on a very specific mission, and follow the instructions given by the university president. Some of these visiting faculty or teachers may be asked by the university to publish their lecture notes and leave them for future reference of the students.

Transcripts The universities keep a very detailed record of all the courses that the students take and the grades they earn.

Counselling the Students Before Each Academic Year Almost a week before each academic year every student is required to see his faculty advisor or counsellor, to decide what courses he needs to take in order to graduate at a certain time. Although the advisor or counsellor is there to help, it is the responsibility of the student to finally select the courses of his interest. The advising is done and the registration is completed before the beginning of the academic year, so that once the year starts, all a student has to do is attend his classes and learn his lessons.

When a faculty advisor is busy, he may ask the student to simply go over the catalog, selecting the courses he wants to take, and see him later. He will then see if everything is alright or not. I remember my first semester at the University of Illinois, when my advisor (a Japanese-American) asked me to do the same. I knew that the University required all Ph.D. candidates to pass a proficiency exam in two foreign languages. I chose

three graduate courses and a French and German course. When my advisor
saw my course selection, he jokingly said I better take Chinese too, as all of
my courses were offered by the Chinese-American professors.

I started the semester with these professors and found it extremely
difficult to understand Professor Chao's accent. I went back to my advisor,
asking him to allow me to drop the course Professor Chao was teaching.
He said this was the case with all the students who take Professor Chao's
classes for the first time. He suggested waiting, and if by the second week I
still had problems with the Professor's accent, then I could drop his course.

By the second week I was already used to Professor Chao's accent and
started to enjoy his lectures greatly. I was so glad to have had a good advisor to help me withdraw my judgement of Professor Chao, for he turned out
to be the best professor I had during my graduate studies at the Universities
of both Wisconsin and Illinois.

How often have I judged a person by very short association, or judged a
book by simply reading the first page, or judged an event before having all
the facts and figures? How often have I judged a society by having known
only one or two of its members?

If I could have only been more patient until I had known the person
better or had more information about the situation, it would have been so
much better. Or, in the case of my courses at the University of Illinois, if I
had only trusted the advice of my advisor, and had taken the courses with
full faith, in the belief that they would be good for me (that they would be
necessary for me to conduct my research and write a successful thesis), I
would have saved myself a lot of discomfort and unhappiness.

The University of Life

Now let us get back to the concept of the University* of Life.

Following is my perception of the life on Earth and the metaphor of the University of Life. This University has its similarities as well as differences with the conventional universities. The University of Life has a campus, a student body, an administration headed by its Master, the supporting staff, programs of study and lessons for all of its students, teaching and research scholarships, academic years and the resting periods, or summer vacation, in between. It also has visiting scholars and lecturers.

Unlike the conventional universities, the University of Life offers only one degree. When a student has completed all the requirements and has sufficiently progressed toward his goal, he will then graduate from this University and will not need to come back to it as a student any more. However, he may come back as an alumni to help special students, in any form that the University Master decides.

Let us now discuss these features briefly. In so doing, I will make an item by item comparison of the University of Life with conventional universities.

The Campus This University (that is, the University of Life) has a campus: it is the whole planet Earth.

The University Administration This University has a Master, and it is God. He, She, or It† has maintained a delicate and highly effective administration. He has appointed some of His friends and the alumni of the University of Life to look after various details for operating this University as efficiently as possible. They do so with total love of the Master, the students, and the campus. Furthermore, they understand the students' capa-

---

*I will be using a capital "U" when I refer to the "University of Life," or "this University."

†There is no gender for God; however, I will use the accepted tradition of "He" and "Him" to refer to God.

bilities and limitations for performing their tasks, and are generally very compassionate in dealing with everything.

The Student Body All the five billion inhabitants on Earth (or this campus) constitute the student body in this University. They are here to learn their lessons and move up to a higher grade or level. It is indeed a large campus with a still large student enrollment. While the size of the campus has remained basically the same, the student enrollment has been increasing constantly.

The Faculty As in the conventional universities, the faculty in this University is also of great significance. If it were not for the dedication of our teachers to teach us what we need to learn, the students (either in the conventional universities or this University) would not be learning their lessons.

The University of Life does not have a separate body called "faculty". This is one difference between the conventional universities and the University of Life. Every student in this University, regardless of age, sex, color, and any other distinction, performs the role of teacher or faculty for one or more of the students. (There are, of course, special or visiting teachers who are appointed for a specific mission. I will refer to them later.) In a sense the University of Life is like a large tutorial institution, where everybody is teaching somebody something, while he himself is learning his lessons from them or someone else.

In many rural areas, where the total student enrollment is low, it is not financially possible to employ teachers for all the grades. Usually one teacher handles several grades in the same room at the same time. I visited one of these schools several years ago in a village south of Iran. There were thirty children in grades one to six, a few preschoolers, and one teacher in the same classroom. The younger ones were there just to be with the rest of the children of the village. Particularly, they did not want to miss the excitement of the school, and wanted to share what they learned each day with their parents when they got home in the afternoon. When I asked the teacher how he managed the teaching, he responded that the students generally teach each other and he is there to help, provide supervision for the class, and teach the sixth graders. I found the students' knowledge quite high for their ages. Furthermore, they were highly motivated.

In the University of Life the lessons are not of a theoretical nature requiring one to memorize them, or comprehend them intellectually. *They are the lessons of life that one learns through experience.* Therefore it is not really necessary that my "teacher" be well versed in the subject matter himself, and to have already passed that lesson. For example the one who provides the opportunity for me to learn patience, does not have to be a patient person himself. The presence of a teacher is merely necessary to provide the opportunities for my experiences, so I can learn.

In this University one learns by exposure, and not through isolation. The more intense the exposure or involvement with other students or teachers, the more one learns. One should never try to isolate himself from the student body or the so-called society by just wanting to live in seclusion, or not to live at all. No one learns anything by spending his time in a cave or on top of a mountain. Besides, by doing so, one also loses his chance for teaching the others their lessons. He thus deprives them of their opportunity to learn and advance in this University.

Because of the duality of the role each person plays in this University, it is therefore impossible to identify the teachers, for everybody is a teacher! Even those who come to this University on special or visiting appointments are difficult to identify. They often remain anonymous, introducing themselves only to their special students.

The Supporting Staff The supporting staff in this University consists of all the things which make life on Earth, or the studying of our lessons, possible. They are: all of the natural resources, with the Sun being the most important of them; all the plants and animals on Earth; the minerals, and so on.

The supporting staff function and carry their responsibilities according to the University Master's plans. While the students at this University need the supporting staff (without whose assistance, hard work, and dedication nothing could be accomplished and no lessons could be learned), it is necessary for the students to appreciate them. The best way to do this is to not disturb them at all, soliciting their help only when there is a need, and only for as much as it is needed. That is, I should not be greedy when it comes to using what the supporting staff (or natural resources) have to offer me, and definitely not waste any, but only use as much as I need.

One other thing which makes the supporting staff very happy is to talk to them. Of course they do not have ears to hear our words, but they can hear very well what comes through our hearts. Just tell them how pretty they are, and thank them for what they are giving us. Tell them that, while they do not need us, we are so much in need of their help. Thank them for just being there when we need them. Acknowledge that if it were not for their help, we would not exist and could not carry out our learning process in this University.

A worry that some of the students in the University of Life have is that there will not be a sufficient number of supporting staff (the so called natural resources) for all of the students. In reality, I believe *it is the appreciation of the supporting staff with which we need to be concerned, not their shortage.* They are willing to give as much as they can, if we only learn how to appreciate their gifts to us, and not to waste or misuse them.

The Degree Offered In the University of Life there is only one degree offered. It is called the "High-God-Awareness," or HGA (like an MBA) Degree.

Receiving this degree does not mean that one has reached his plateau of God awareness. There is indeed no limit to God awareness. The degree simply means that the student does not need to come back to this University (unless as a special teacher) to reach a higher level of God awareness. This is very similar to the degree offered by the conventional universities. Receiving a doctorate degree from these universities, for example, does not mean that the student is through learning. It simply means that the university does not have any more to offer this person to advance his knowledge in the field he has been pursuing.

The Program of Study and the Lessons The programs of study and lessons in this University are tailor-made; no two students have identical programs of study, and no two students are taking the same courses, or studying the same lessons.

Before starting a new academic year in this University, each student reviews his entire transcript with the Master (through one or more of His friends), and with their assistance he chooses his program of study, including all courses, laboratories, and the field trips that he needs to take. Their objective is that the students finish his lessons and receive his HGA Degree as soon as possible. Receiving this degree may take several thousands of such academic years. But the students have complete freedom in their studies. They can take it easy and spend a lot of time learning a given lesson and finishing a program of study, or take more difficult courses. This is somewhat like the conventional universities where, for example, a student may spend three to twenty years to receive a bachelor of science degree.

I remember when I was taking a German course to fulfill one of the requirements of my Ph. D. program at the University of Illinois. The policy was either to pass two special German courses with grades B or better, or pass the proficiency exam of that language. I decided to take the first course and at the end of the semester try the proficiency exam. I took this course with a professor who was known for being very tough, and giving a lot of homework. With what I learned in this course alone, I was able to pass the proficiency exam. So, by working a little harder during the first few months of the semester, I saved myself much time and advanced my graduation date a little.

In the University of Life, when a student feels that he has wasted a lot of time in the previous academic years and wants to "catch up," he may want to sign up for more difficult courses, or take a heavier study load than most students do.

In my university teaching experience, I have seen many of my students wanting to take a heavier study load than normal, or wanting to skip the prerequisite courses, or take certain proficiency examinations in order to graduate sooner. They argue that they want to graduate by a certain date, and that they can work harder to overcome the deficiencies that they have in certain areas. I normally advise them and discuss with them the nature of the courses that they are interested in, telling them that it is their choice; that they are responsible for their studies, and I am only here to help them.

The Scholarship There are no tuitions and fees in the University of Life. Furthermore, room and board are also provided free. However, as part of their studies, students need to make some effort in helping the supporting staff for the final preparation of their food, clothing, shelter, etc.

Actually, the most essential elements such as air and the solar radiation are absolutely free. These are available to the students all the time, and they do not have to do anything to use them. However, when elements such as air and solar radiation are given to us free, we feel obligated to do something. That is, either to help the supporting staff be themselves, or just help the other students study better in this University.

When the students' needs for certain things (such as water, food, clothing, etc.) become less crucial, the students will have to make some effort to prepare them for their use. They are provided free, but often not exactly in the same form that the students are comfortable or capable of using them in. For many students the preparation of food, clothing, shelter, etc., is a means for learning their lessons and reaching their goal or receiving their HGA Degree sooner.

The Admission Policies An entity on planet Earth who has attained the highest level of God awareness in the animal kingdom may be admitted to the University of Life. There are also transfer students from other planets. It is the University Master who sets the admission policies and decides about the admission of each student.

The Examinations and the Probationary Policies There are no announced dates for the examinations. Throughout an academic year quizzes of short duration which cover only a few subjects, or more comprehensive examinations covering many areas and lasting for a longer time, may be administered for each student. These exams are given to see if a student has mastered a certain lesson. They usually provide excellent additional learning opportunities for each student.

In my teaching experience at the conventional universities I have always made sure that the students learned at least as much from their exams as they did from my lectures. It normally took me a longer time to prepare these exams, but I thought it was worth it. Many students did not like this approach, saying that exams should be intended only to test their knowledge. On the other hand, there were many other students who liked the challenge of learning new things. My argument was that the entire time we have been together in the classroom has been a learning opportunity for all of us. I chose to call some of these time slots "lecture hours," and the others, "examination periods."

As a student in the University of Life, I know when I am learning a lesson and when I am taking an examination. After reading an article or a book, or listening to lectures dealing with spiritual matters such as forgiveness, love, complete surrender to the will of God, accepting a person as he is, or a situation as it has happened (that is, without any expectations), trusting God to provide anything that I need, believing that everyone I love and tend to worry about is really in good hands and I need not worry, and so on, I tell myself that now I have learned the lessons. Then comes, in the most subtle way, a little quiz, in the form of meeting someone, witnessing an event, losing something, etc., where I am tested to see if I have indeed learned the lesson, *or if I have just spent some time with the issue, having had only an intellectual experience.* These intellectual learning processes are very much similar to my learning how to swim. I may spend a lot of time studying the hydrodynamics of swimming. But the real learning comes when I jump into the water and do it! It is during this practical activity that I not only learn to improve my swimming, but am also tested for my swimming skills.

Consulting with the University Master It is with these short and long examinations in the University of Life that I realize how far I have to go yet to master all the lessons I need and have agreed to learn. When I see my grades and realize that I need to improve my studying habits, I decide to do something about it. I feel a need to see a counsellor, or better yet, to go and see the University Master Himself. I know some students who, in similar situations as mine, prefer to see one of God's friends, or one of the University Administrators. However, I prefer to go to the Master directly.

I want to see the University Master to acknowledge my shortcomings in my studies. I want to acknowledge that "I, by my own self, can do nothing." I want to beg of Him to please help me and show me how best I can learn my lessons in this University.

The University Master or God has an "open door policy," and everyone can go to Him and talk to Him *any time he chooses*. This is not the case with conventional universities, where one can hardly even get past the secretary of the university president. But this University's Master is actually never busy, and always has time to receive the needy students. One doesn't even have to make any appointment to see Him.

However, to see the Master I need to do some preparation. Have you ever seen people going for a job interview? They are in their best appearances, wearing their best clothing, showing a great deal of confidence, and smiling constantly. They know that their appearance helps them in their landing a job.

Several years ago when I was a visiting professor at the University of Waterloo in Canada, I needed to hire a student to help me with my research for the summer. The university's policy required that all such job opportunities be properly advertised so that all qualified students could apply. After complying with the university's rules, and selecting ten students (from a list of seventy applicants) for an interview, the students came to see me one by one. Nine of these students were the ones I already had in my classes. They used to come to their classes with completely casual clothing. But on the day of their interview they were all dressed in their best; they were smiling constantly, each demonstrating to me that he or she was very interested in my work, and that he or she would be the best choice for the job.

Similarly, to get the University Master's attention and land a favor from Him, I also need to become presentable. For one thing, He doesn't really care about my clothing or anything superficial. What He really likes is my complete surrender and trust in Him. More than anything He likes me to be humble. He does not like to deal with arrogant students who, although wanting to see the University Master and ask for help, end up telling Him what He needs to do, or how He should run His University. When seeing the University Master, *I know that the more humble I am, the easier it is to reach Him.* It is as if by becoming a truly humble entity I can then dial His personal number and bypass all the obstacles which existed between Him and me.

I know I can reach that state of humility when I actually do not see other students or teachers as separate from myself, and from Him. That is, I grow to perceive only one thing: God. We are all Him. It is not me, you, him, her, them, or whatever, it is only one thing and it is God. When I reach the state of awareness that I am actually with God all the time, that He is not in a far away place in the sky (referred to by many people as "heaven") but right here, in me. Where I am, God is, and this becomes my reality.

I know that when I reach that level of God awareness, I am ready to graduate from this University. As long as I do not have this awareness I keep coming back to learn more lessons. At least I now know that I can go to see the University Master anytime I need some assistance with my studies. He is indeed The Professor, while all other teachers are just the tutors. Now I have learned that to see the Master, I have to drop all my ideas of separateness with all the five billion students, and billions and billions of staff members, in this University.

He has made it clear that actually He is closer to us than we are to ourselves (what is closer to a person than that, except being the person himself!), and can always be seen and communicated with by anyone. *The reason that I do not or can not communicate with Him is because I have built so many walls and shields around me that the lines of sight and sound to Him are obstructed.* He tells me that if I break all the walls, then I will have no difficulty communicating with Him and feeling His presence in me. The reason that I do not see all things as God is because I am "cross-eyed." I need to improve my vision, and when I do, I will see all things as one Divine Entity.

When I go to see the University Master, He wants me to go alone; free like a soaring bird, with no attachments. Not like a clumsy crab which, because of its fears, covers itself with so many pebbles and debris so it can hardly move about. He wants me to be free of excess baggage: the things that I have acquired throughout the years, and have become so attached to, that I think I can't live without them. These are things like position, wealth, family ties, pride for being different and being separate from the rest of the student body, pride that I was born in such and such a place, or my fathers were so and so; prides of being of a certain race, or religious attachment, and even pride of a certain nationality.

He likes the students to be completely devoid of their egos, with total humility, and with no arrogance whatsoever. It is only when I go before Him free like a bird and with nothing attached to me to hinder my flight, that I get to hear Him. The education that I have received and may be proud of, my accomplishments in serving mankind (for example, the humanitarian thoughts that I have saved millions and millions of people from a certain disease, or famine, let's say) will not help me have my wishes granted by Him. Especially if I *have* done any of these, I do not consider myself as the one who did them, nor do I deserve recognition. I consider God as having accomplished them, but *through* me. I thank him for making me the instrument for such creative actions.

What should I wish when I am so near Him and feeling His presence in my whole self? Should I ask for health, wealth, position, success in overcoming a certain problem, eliminating famine, diseases, and injustices from the face of the planet, or what? Really, what shall I ask Him, or what request shall I make of Him, that He doesn't already know? He knows what all our needs are. When I am so near Him and am feeling His presence in me, how can I remember what to ask? I have become so absorbed by His love, majesty, and greatness, that in His presence I forget all of these and become one with Him. I forget that I have sometimes felt separate from Him. Actually I forget that I had come to ask Him for anything.

I know that feeling His presence in me is the greatest gift I can ask Him to give me. But, I will make one daring request and ask Him to please give the same gift to the other students of this University. I know He will, if the students only know how to go to Him and ask; not to go to far away places searching for Him, but to reach Him right inside themselves. We can reach Him through quiet moments of meditation and prayer, when all ideas of separateness are cast aside. These are moments when one stills his thoughts and only listens.

Actually, the idea of oneness is the main lesson that we are learning in the University of Life. The Master knows that we do not learn it during one or two academic years. He knows that it takes time, but He has given us the freedom to choose our own pace. In a given academic year, if a student does not learn his lessons well, or does not pass a certain examination or many exams, he is not "flunked out" of this University. These students will be sent back to this University again and again until they learn their lessons and graduate.

The Academic Years and the Summer Vacations   Unlike the conventional universities which follow a definite calendar and have a fixed academic year for all the students, the length of the academic year in the University of Life is not fixed; it varies from one student to another. It may be as short as a few minutes or hours, or it may go up to several decades.

After completing one academic year, or life span, there comes a summer vacation — the transition to another plane — or what the majority of people call "death." During this period the individuals (or entities) have entirely different life styles and activities. For one thing, they are not bound by the gravity of Earth and can move around quite easily (particularly when they are in graduate standing in this University).

Not too many people quite know what is happening on this plane. It appears to me that there are regions, zones, or spheres to accommodate the summer vacationers. These zones do not have physical boundaries. Therefore, we cannot easily visualize them. They are separated only by levels of consciousness. Depending on the class standing in the academic year, which is really a representative of one's level of God awareness, the students will be assigned to various regions or zones. In other words, (borrowing terminologies from conventional universities) the freshmen students will be accommodated together, the sophomores together, the seniors together, the graduate students together, and so on.

The ones at lower class standing, being limited in their God awareness have less joy and see the grandeur of Creation in a very limited way. They feel surrounded by less of God's light. On the other hand, the ones with higher class standing, or higher God awareness (like seniors as compared with the freshmen in the conventional universities) are more thrilled with the majesty of Creation and therefore feel surrounded by more light of God. They enjoy their summer vacation more.

The extent of the enjoyment of these entities is so high that the lower classmen, seeing all the fun these students have, become jealous and want this, too. It is here that they are told: in order for them to attain this level of joy and happiness, or to move from one zone of pleasure to the one higher, they need to go back to the University of Life and learn more lessons in another academic year. The counsellors, by reviewing the students' transcripts, point out to them where they stand academically in the University, and what they need to do, or what courses they need to take. The choice is, of course, the students'. They are never forced to do anything. In seeing all the fun the upper classmen have, and how miserable they themselves have been, they often choose to come back and take tough lessons.

The duration of summer vacation is not the same for everyone. Some will have a short summer holiday, and some may take several years. But they will all come back to the University to spend another academic year to learn more, and move on toward their final objective — to receive their High-God-Awareness Degree.

It is indeed during this summer vacation that each student becomes aware of his standing in the University. When he realizes how far he has to go, and sees all the good things which are happening to the graduate students and how much fun they have, he becomes upset, annoyed, and sometimes totally miserable (as if being in "hell!"). He thinks about all the time he wasted when he could have been studying. He also realizes that going back for more academic years would be the only way to transcend his miseries. All the students are made aware of the Master's plan and are assured that they will eventually graduate from the University.

Those students who are farther advanced in their studies have great times, yet still see the blissful time the ones above them have. They all see the great joy that God awareness has brought those above and see the light which surrounds them. Association with those who have finished their studies and have attained their degrees gives them such a pleasure that they, too, want to come back to receive the same degree sooner. Now that they are more aware of what is going on, they may even choose some tough lessons and follow an exceptionally difficult program of study during their next academic year in order to hasten their graduation from the University of Life. They all strive to have constant companionship with God or the University Master.

Whatever courses the students have decided to take when they return to this University, they still have freedom of choice to follow them or take other courses which result in the same learning experience.

Access to the Students' Transcripts and Plans of Study Generally one's transcript and plan of study are kept confidential in this University. However, there may be found a few individuals with special talents (normally called psychic) who may see part of a student's transcript, or vaguely see the student's plan of study for his current academic year. Of course the visiting professors or masters, who have special missions on campus and live among the students, have better access to such information.

But they will never reveal such information to other students. They obtain this knowledge in order to help their special students more.

It is also possible for some students to access such information about themselves or other students, in their dreams. I know of several such events, particularly one involving an automobile accident and the death of three people, which friends or relatives had forseen in their dreams.

What appears to me is that even if such information is revealed, that is, even if a student finds out what courses he has planned to take, he is not bound or obligated to follow it. He can always change his mind; follow a new study program and take new courses.

Several years ago, I loaned some money to a man after he was involved in a motorcycle accident, could not work, and had no income for several weeks. The day after, the school bus bringing my daughter home from her kindergarten was involved in an accident which could have been very serious. Fortunately she and the other children had only small bruises. The same night I saw Haji Kamal (the teacher mentioned in chapter two) at his house in one of the sessions he used to hold. As soon as he saw me he asked what did I do the day before which eliminated a serious danger from a member of my family. I had to think for a while to remember the event of the day and what I had done the day before. He then went on to discuss how important it is to help those in need, no matter what the help is. He pointed out that actually we can reduce or eliminate many difficulties, dangers, or miseries in our lives by simply helping people. The more unselfish the deed, the more significant will be the reward.

Special Guidelines or How-To-Study Books Students are often encouraged to take special "how-to-study" courses, or follow a certain guideline, in order to improve their study habits. Then, they can handle several really tough courses during one academic year and advance their graduation date. These "how-to-study" courses are actually taught by those alumni or special teachers who come to the University with only visiting appointments. Many of these master teachers, or visiting professors, leave their lecture notes and books behind for the students to follow. In some cases, where the master teacher did not prepare any written notes himself, some of the students in his class may later prepare notes from memory. These books, or teachings, as they are often called, are like the maps of a city which one may want to follow in order to reach his destination sooner. The students have, of course, free will to follow these masters (called prophets and men of God) or just wander around on their own.

The teachings of these prophets or sages, while pure in their original form and intended for the benefit of the students of this University, have often been distorted and polluted by selfish, ignorant, unenlightened students. This is akin to a child taking a text book written for the benefit of the students in a conventional university and drawing all kinds of lines in it, cutting off some pages, or in general, distorting the content of the book.

These undergraduate students get ahold of these books or lecture notes, and because of their physical or social power in the society, and because of their utmost selfishness, appoint themselves as the guardians of the teachings and start altering them to their liking. They interpret the teachings of the masters for their own benefit. Eventually, the original lecture notes or book become completely distorted, so that they no longer provide any guidance for the students. After a while, many students give up reading these polluted "how-to-study" books altogether. The University Master, being aware of this phenomenon, may choose to send another master teacher or visiting professor, not only to clarify these distortions, eliminating the pollution, but also to provide a more detailed "how-to-study" book. Comparing it again to the map of a city, this now becomes a more detailed map to help people reach their destinations sooner.

Freedom of Choice Always Prevails Every student has complete freedom to select his courses or the program of study *during* summer vacation. He may even replace them with easier or harder courses during the academic year. But he is eager to have fun while studying, and wants to finish his program of study as soon as possible. This way, when he returns for summer vacation, he will have more fun than he had when he was there last. He wants to enjoy the pleasant and beautiful environment that God, the University Master, has provided for the students according to their University standing and level. Furthermore, he does not want to come back to this University again and does not want to carry around a heavy mass, called body, as his study kit.

In returning to the University for another academic year, it is possible for many students to decide to come back together, follow a somewhat similar program of study and learn their lessons together. It is also possible that they, as good friends from vacation times, give each other really difficult challenges to make sure their lessons are learned and progress is secured. However, once on campus, they do not recognize each other. They do not remember their agreements, and sometimes become furious with one another for the hard time they are having.

I remember reading about two traffic judges in Europe who were riding their bicycles at night without having their lights on. They were stopped by a policeman and were cited for violating a certain state ordinance. They looked at each other with surprise, then decided: well it would be only fair if they treated one another as violators of the law, and as if they did not know each other.

The next day, John appeared before George as a defendant and pleaded guilty to the charges. George then fined him five dollars. When George appeared before John, he was fined ten dollars for his offense. George seeing the unfairness became upset and said, "I fined you five dollars for this offense, so why are you charging me ten?" John, acting as if he did not know George at all, replied, "This is the second case we have had this morning of this nature, and we need to put an end to it by raising the fine."

At the time when the program of study is decided upon, the students may also decide who their teachers will be during the next academic year. That is, before starting a new academic year (or new life) each one of us has already planned the courses to take, where to take them, and with whom to take them.

The Forgetful Students Although every student has selected his program of study when he starts the new academic year, he forgets all about it and becomes angry at the people who (also not knowing why they are doing what they are doing) are seemingly giving him hard times. In reality, *these people are trying to teach him lessons that he himself has agreed to take in order to progress.* The student is so unaware of what he has agreed to before, that he becomes furious about his predicaments. It is only the graduate students in this University who remember some of what they had previously agreed upon. Furthermore, these students value their teachers, and do not call the events in their lives "accidents," as the undergraduate students do. The graduate students simply call them lessons of life and enjoy taking them. They are grateful to their teachers, particularly the ones who are giving them tough assignments.

Summary

The concepts presented so far may be summarized as follows:

1. **Purpose** Every one of us, regardless of age, sex, skin color, place of origin, and what we do for a living, has been created for a purpose, which is to become fully aware of God's presence in everything. This is not by bringing God into our lives, since He is already there, but rather by becoming aware of what we truly are: manifestations or faces of the Divine Power.

2. **Method of Reaching Our Goal** We reach our goal, fulfilling our purpose or mission in life by going through the University of Life. Here, we learn certain lessons which eventually make us believe in the power we have possessed all along, without being aware of it. This is like a child who inherits millions of dollars, but because of his age is not aware of his wealth. When he reaches a mature age he finds out that he has been a millionaire all along, without knowing it.

3. **Dual Role of Student and Teacher** We are all students in this University of Life. Every person in our life plays an important role of being a teacher for us, and we in turn act as teachers for others.

4. **Our Lessons** No matter what we do and whom we are with, we are constantly learning and teaching. We never stand still in this learning and growth. This we do, not by just memorizing certain rituals or the sayings of prophets and sages. *Rather, by faithfully accepting certain principles and by putting them into practice.* Our transformation requires experience plus ACTION. This we do, not just during one life time of only a few years or decades, but by coming back to this University, taking new courses, and being exposed to new experiences. The marvel of this educational system is that no two students have identical programs of study or are taking the same lessons at the same time. Everything is tailor made for each student.

5. **The Degree Awarded in this University** Our going through the University of Life results in the Degree of High God Awareness. This degree is awarded once we have reached the state in which we experience only one thing: God.

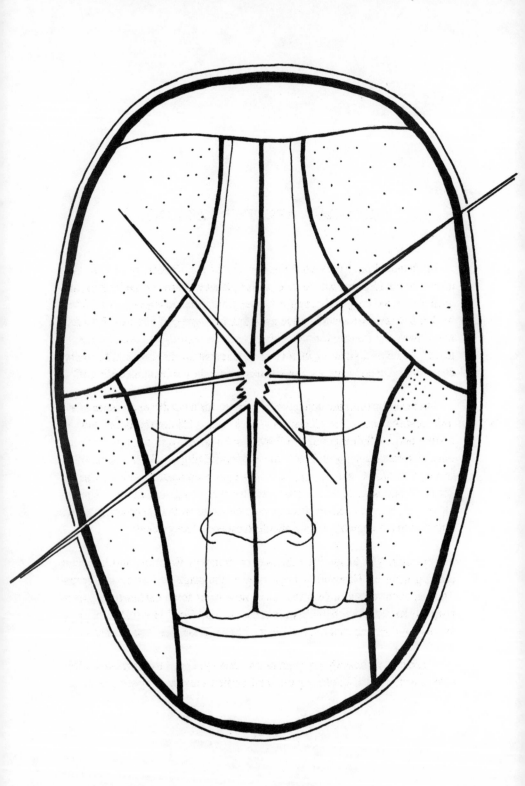

5. WHAT ARE THE LESSONS?

In chapter four I presented the concept of the University of Life, and discussed the idea that we are here on this planet to learn certain lessons, and until we do, we keep returning for further education and experiences. When we learn these lessons we will be awarded the Degree of High God Awareness. Now the question is this: what are these lessons that we are here to learn? Are they something that we need to memorize or learn intellectually, as we do in the conventional universities, or are they something different?

I believe the ultimate objective or purpose for us is the *acceptance of the unity and the oneness of all creatures with God.* This is the belief that all people and all living beings on Earth (and elsewhere in the universe) are only manifestations, or different faces of one Entity: God. It is God Who, in the drama of Creation, *appears* as people, as plants, as animals, as insects, as the planets, as the stars, and as everything that exists. That is, everything we see or know through our senses, as well as everything we do not see and are unaware of, is a manifestation or a face of God.

It is God Who has written the play or drama of Creation, and has been playing it all by Himself — appearing as the stage and as all the props. That is, every creature (whether alive now or at some earlier time), from prophets to little insects, viruses, plants, etc., is "God" Himself, appearing as such and playing that role. He is it. The universe is a "one God show."

As an entity presently unaware of my identity, I need to learn certain lessons, starting with simple experiences, or first playing simple roles of the

41

drama. Then, I learn harder lessons, go through tougher experiences of life, and play more difficult roles. This process continues. In passing through all these experiences in life, *I get closer and closer to Home. I begin to identify myself with that Divine Source, and start feeling our oneness.* It is through these experiences that I come to realize that everyone else is *also* playing a role. I find that we are essentially the **same**, and not different. We are just playing the roles our Playwright has assigned us, and we are manifestations of Him.

To reach this level of belief, and to experience the feeling of oneness with all people and all things, *I need to gradually increase my level of awareness.* This is like starting from the bottom and moving up the ladder of perfection. On each step of this ladder (or the academic year of the University of Life) I have to interact with other people, and expose myself to what they are here to teach me. I do not gain anything if I simply choose to isolate myself from the excitement of life, and divorce the world. I know that everything the other creatures do to me is part of the drama that they are playing, and is helpful for their growth as well.

Somewhere in this ladder which leads me to a complete reunion with the Creator, I will be awarded the Degree of High God Awareness in the University of Life. After this, I do not need to come to this planet any more, except to return as a special teacher such as a prophet, saint, or man of God. From then on, I will continue evolving in God awareness, as such awareness is limitless. This, however, will occur on more advanced planes.

The lessons of this world are not something I memorize. They are the things I need to experience and incorporate as parts of my belief system. I sense what will happen when I reach the high level of God awareness. I will lose all senses of separateness, and feel one with all people and all things. This happens when I drop any distinction between people because of color, age, sex, their place of birth or residence, the type of work they do, etc. It happens when I look at all the people in the world as my brothers and sisters, and all other creatures such as plants, animals, insects, etc., as my "cousins." It happens when I accept that these creatures also have their own lives to live, and they, too, are evolving into a greater level of God awareness.

It is such a wonderful feeling to be one with the universe, with my brothers and sisters and all of my cousins. *Then I am one with the Master.*

6. LOOKING AT EVENTS IN LIGHT OF THE UNIVERSITY OF LIFE

In chapter two I shared several events with you. They basically dealt with people who had hard times in their lives. One can think of many examples where people, although poor, live their lives in total peace and serenity. These families are not always noticeable, however. On the other hand, there are people, although wealthy, who never seem to have enough, and always complain. We see people who are ill and live through it, and we also see people who are healthy and wealthy, but always discontent.

Let us look at the example of the baby girl, Maryam, who went blind and no doctor could figure out the cause, nor offer any cure. Let us look at this event in the context of the University of Life. To me the event was simply a series of lessons needing to be learned by many people, including the baby herself, who would learn much from it when she grew up. Let me now summarize some of the positive points in the incident:

1. The parents by becoming heart-broken and by not being able to find a medical solution for the problem *became closer to God,* and deep in their hearts they asked Him for help. The same was true with the whole community who shared the grief of the young couple and the baby.

2. The medical field, not being able to solve the problem, now had a topic of significance to investigate and research. If it had not been for all those people who got sick and perhaps died throughout history, the fields of science and medicine would not have progressed to their present level.

45

For many people, learning about nature and the human body becomes an excellent means of getting closer to God.

3. Attention was paid to the fact that there are very advanced souls who know what is going on in life, can forsee the future, and predict events. This provided an excellent opportunity to demonstrate that it is not just through science that we become aware of our environment and predict certain outcomes, as the medical doctors do. We can also find out about our surroundings by tapping the Universal Mind, or God. He is all knowing; therefore one can tap, if he only learns how, this Universal source of knowledge. This is very much like dialing a number to hear a weather report. Weather bureaus now store such data in computers, and services are available to report the weather throughout the world by telephone. God, the source of all knowledge, is also accessible through special "numbers." Those who reach a certain level of God awareness are given some of these "toll-free" numbers.

4. A lot of financial assistance was rendered to the poor. While Ali, the baby's father, was basically a generous man and used to give a lot to charities, he would never have given the amounts he did if it were not for his daughter's condition. There are times in life, under dire conditions, when we are willing to give everything we have, in order to restore the health of a beloved one. This is particularly true in the case of children. I am sure that if you were a millionaire and your child had gone blind you would have been more than willing to give all you owned to restore the child's sight. When your child is well and fine, isn't it like being a millionaire?

5. It brought a sense of gratitude to God for what people had, particularly the health they were enjoying.

With this example and many others I have witnessed in my life, I have come to believe that events of life never have a single purpose. Or, from the context of the University of Life, no lesson is designed just for one person to learn. For every event there are lessons to be learned by many people, in both the present and the future. (Such as my presenting the case of Maryam here and sharing it with you).

I believe that Maryam's blindness was not just an accident. It comprised a series of lessons for many people to learn. It is impossible for me to see the full extent of the impact this event has had, and the learning process involved for people who experienced or witnessed it. I have already shared some of them. During her six months of blindness, Maryam acted as a teacher, and taught many lessons to many people. To her parents and many close to the family, she taught the lessons of patience and faith. She proved that material wealth is a trust from God to us: and that we must share it with others, especially those in need, before life forces us to spend it for medical expenses.

Tithing ten percent of my income, or sharing what I have with the poor, can bring me joy and happiness. I feel joyful to contribute, and to have been an instrument of God in sharing His bounty with others. What is amazing is that generosity and tithing can actually prevent or divert various problems. This is very difficult to verify scientifically. However, I have had both personal experience and the intuition that by helping someone, a member of *my* family was spared from a bus accident which could have been fatal. Only minor injuries were sustained.

The courses in the University of Life are planned for many purposes. A "course" such as Maryam's blindness, demonstrated that while all other doors were closed, there existed the direct door to God, which remained open. This door is available for anyone to knock on at any time. If our knock is earnest and our request sincere, He will surely answer. Maryam's blindness also provided a lesson about how insignificant in the greater picture our material wealth is. We learn that by giving it away and sharing it with those in need, our cup "runneth over."

I can enumerate many lessons available from other events described in chapter two. It might be helpful for you to list your own experiences, and discover some of life's lessons for you!

Exercise

List an event you have witnessed in your life, and list all the lessons you, and those involved, may have learned from it.

7. HOW TO STUDY IN THIS UNIVERSITY

About three years ago when I was invited to go to Milan, Italy, to attend a conference, I was surprised when I found out that the conference organizers had not received my letter, did not know the time of my arrival, and therefore could not meet me at the airport. I found a hotel near the central train station, and decided to reach my destination by taking the airport bus to the station, and then a taxi from there to my hotel. I figured that this would be less expensive than taking a taxi directly from the airport to the hotel.

Arriving at the train station, I told the first taxi driver in the waiting line where I wanted to go. He suggested I could walk, as it was very near. He pointed out the general direction of the hotel. I thanked him and started walking in that direction. After asking another person, I finally found my hotel. I did not have a map to find my way, and asking people for directions was the only way to find my final destination.

Later that night a question came to my mind. I wondered what would have happened if there had been nobody to help me to reach my destination. I knew I would have eventually found the place. Without having a vehicle, I would have had to walk through all the streets in town, looking for the name of my hotel, and moving on, street by street, until I found it. Without a map or anyone to help, and assuming that I could remember all the streets I had already passed, it would have taken me, perhaps, a year to reach my destination. But eventually I would have found it. With the help of a few people whose assistance I could trust, it took me only a few minutes. Of course, it would have been even more convenient if I could have taken the taxi to reach my destination.

In this University of Life, where each one of us is simultaneously both student and teacher, and everyone is working for the final Degree of High God Awareness, one can learn his lessons in several ways. Some choose to learn them haphazardly, while others follow the "tips" and directions given to them. These are provided by the University Master through the visiting professors. These special teachers are those sent by Him to this University on special assignments.

My studying at the University of Life is very much like my wandering around in the streets of Milan to reach my destination. This could easily have taken me about a year to accomplish, but by following the city map (after I had learned to read it), and following the tips given by people I could trust, I arrived safely in a short time. In the University of Life, the choice is mine: to take the direct, efficient route (the "straight and narrow path"), or the haphazard route. This choice is up to each of us.

Tips on How to Study in this University

What are the tips which will help me study my lessons more effectively, and reach my final "destination" sooner, and with the least trouble?

The following are tips which will help me learn my lessons better. I believe they are the essence of the teachings of all religions of the world.

1. The belief that this world or the University of Life has a Master, and He is in total control of every event in His University. Furthermore, He has designed every program of study, every lesson, every class schedule, and all instructional materials. He has even appointed specific teachers for each student.

2. Because of the Master's total and absolute involvement in all the affairs of this University, everything operates by Divine Order. There is absolutely nothing bad, ugly, or wrong in this University, and thus we need not be in judgement of the curriculum or the people. This includes the lessons, the schedules of classes, the way the teachers teach their subject matter to the students, the way each student has chosen to learn his lessons, and even the way the teachers and students (including myself) behave, think, or look. From this perspective everything becomes acceptable, understandable, systematic, and orderly.

3. The belief that every person in my life is performing the valuable task of teaching me lessons to attain my High-God-Awareness Degree sooner. I acknowledge the work of my teachers, and thank and love them for their role in teaching me what I need to learn. I realize that they go through a great deal of hardship, particularly when they teach me tough lessons, and that this requires time, effort, and dedication on their part.

4. Realization that the hard and painful lessons I am learning are really part of the University's *"honor's program,"* and by my willing participation I will be eligible for a major award. This happens when my performance is reviewed by the University Master during my summer vacation.

5. Trust in the University Master that everything is just fine in the University. That trust is appropriate, even though I may temporarily feel unhappy about a teacher, a program of study, particular lesson, classroom setting, or anything else.

6. Giving of my total and unconditional love to other students and faculty. My love therefore embraces the way they are: the way they behave, think, study their lessons, or even look. I will remain non-critical of myself and love myself as well. I come to realize that, after all, everything is created by God, the University Master. Since everything is a face or manifestation of God, it cannot be anything but beautiful. I learn to behold beauty everywhere and in everything.

7. A relationship with the University Master permeates my life. I constantly keep in touch with Him, begging Him to show me how best I may teach my students, and perform my duties in His University. I beg Him to give me the ability to totally submit and surrender myself to His plans, knowing that "I, by my own self, can do nothing." I ask Him to help me just follow His wishes. I request Him to give me the ability to love Him, love myself, and love my fellow students fully and unconditionally.

It is such a beautiful experience when one "hears and receives" God's messages. These messages do not have to (and often do not) come in the form of a letter, telegram, or telephone call. They do not advertise as, "this is God talking, responding to your request." This may come, if God so wishes, in the form of a feeling, thought, vision, voice, and in many other ways. One has to be aware, open, and trusting for the message to come. If nothing comes immediately, we must not get impatient, but wait. All things come in time. Patience, receptivity, and a true humility are our spiritual doors to success.

You may have heard or read about a pious man who always trusted God to take care of him and protect him against dangers. One spring when the rainfall was more than the city sewage system could handle and the streets were being flooded, the city officials decided to evacuate the people to higher and safer grounds. They first informed everyone of the expected rainfall and the forthcoming flood, asking people to leave their homes. Many did. This man, believing that God would take care of him, did not leave, and stayed behind. The rain flooded the streets, and those who were left behind were evacuated by boats. The man refused to go along with the plan and stayed behind, saying that God had promised to save His pious servants. The water reached his roof level and he had to climb to the top of his house to avoid drowning and to wait for God's miracles to save him. A helicopter came to his rescue, but he still refused to go along, saying he was awaiting God's help.

When the flood finally drowned him, he met God with anger, accusing Him of promising to save His servants and not following through. God told him, "I sent you the warning to evacuate, you refused; I sent you the boat to take you away to a safer ground, you refused; I sent you a helicopter to save you, you still refused. What else did you expect me to do?"

God speaks to us through the medium of events and human interaction. This occurs through people. We can say, then, that God's messages reach us through all the avenues of life. As we become more aware, we sense the unseen hand of God behind all events in the physical world.

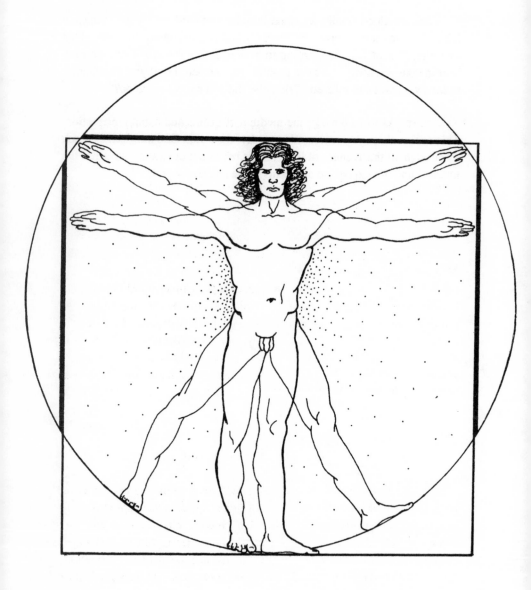

8. MY STUDY KIT IN THIS UNIVERSITY

In the University of Life I am both a student and a teacher. I am here to learn certain lessons and move on to the next level. I then study and learn the lessons of that level and progress further. While studying I will also help others learn their lessons and move on in their studies. After mastering my lessons I will graduate from this University and will receive my Degree of High God Awareness or HGA. In this University no one can "flunk out." There does not seem to be any place for the University Master to send the "naughty" students. He keeps sending them back to this University until they make it, eventually receiving their HGA degree. How long it takes to receive this degree depends mostly on the students' efforts. Furthermore, in this University the entire program of study is tailor-made to the students' needs. The courses we teach and the things we do are largely pre-arranged. No two students have identical programs.

Need for a Study Kit

As a student in the University of Life, I need to have a certain kit to work through. In the conventional educational systems there are also study kits such as chemistry kits, physics kits, sewing kits, cooking kits, etc. When the Master designed this University and started admitting students to its programs, He also designed their kits. Just like the students themselves, no two kits are identical, although they may look alike. Because the Master

loved His University and its students and faculty so much, He decided to
design the best kit possible for them.

The Kits' Various Functions

These kits, while being very beautiful, also serve several purposes. One
of the functions of each kit is to be a vehicle, and carry the student or
teacher around. Another function is to communicate with the other kits.
The kits are also very intelligent and can actually think. But their most
important function is, of course, to be used simply as the study kit in this
University of Life.

The kits serving as vehicles is similar to college students having a
means of transportation to reach their classes in conventional universities.
For example, I have seen students travelling to class on bicycles (riding
alone or sitting on the handle bars), skate boards, in cars of all sizes and
shapes, and even some on horseback.

In the University of life, our "vehicles" are also very different from one
another. Some are large, some small, some white, some black, some old
and some new. But they are all being used to carry the students/teachers
around.

Businesses Tending to the Needs of the Kits

In conventional universities there are lots of businesses around campus
tending to the needs of students' vehicles. There are service stations, bicycle
shops, etc. (but no more shops caring for horses). In this University the
maintenance of the kits has also become a thriving business. The study of
these kits, or "kitology," and learning how to fix them when something
goes wrong (which happens often, due to misuse) is a big business. For
some people it has even become part of their curriculum and lessons.

Other Features of the Kits

There are many interesting things about the kits in this University. For one thing, these kits have genders and come in male and female models. This is quite different from the sewing kits, cooking kits, or even chemistry and physics kits in the regular educational systems. As vehicles, they are also different from the ones the students use to get around their campuses. For example, the kits of the opposite sex in this University can actually reproduce and come up with little ones which they simply call babies. Wouldn't it be nice if the vehicles in conventional universities could also reproduce — particularly when they make head on collisions — to create baby cars?

Other beautiful things about these kits are that every minute part of each kit is constantly changing and regenerating. It also has a great ability to repair itself. For these reasons you can find kits from the World War I era, but you don't find too many vehicles in conventional universities still in operation that long.

The Love of the Kits

The kits in this University love their baby kits so much. In fact, through experiencing unconditional love for them, this experience alone becomes, for many students, a means of learning in-depth lessons, thus moving on in their studies.

The Kits' Needs

For all the functions these kits have, and for transporting the students wherever they want to go, the kits need energy. This is the first law of thermodynamics, a subject I have taught for many years. The same applies to vehicles in conventional universities. They, too, need energy input to operate and also need attention and care for their well being. Ironically, the students in the University of Life seem to be less careful about their kit-vehicles than the students in conventional universities. They often mistreat them either by using the wrong fuel, or with improper maintenance. Some even damage them with the kinds of abuse students in conventional universities would never consider (skateboards excepted!)

There are also problems with these kits. The worst difficulty the undergraduate students have is that they have forgotten that these are *just kits,* given to each one of us to study and teach through. We use them to "get on with life." Students become so absorbed by the marvels of the kits that they confuse *Themselves* with their kits.

My Kit

My kit is so beautiful and demands so little of me. It mostly takes care of itself and combats my mistreating or abusing it. When I really have mistreated it, it simply complains and gives me signals, which the undergraduate students in this University call pains and illnesses. These *signals* are requests from my kit to me, sometimes asking in the most subtle way, for me to be gentle. Particularly, it asks that I not refuel it with junk foods, junk drinks, polluted air, and especially junk thoughts. It simply wants me to care for it, pay attention to it, love it, and be respectful to it.

I love my kit. It is my body. I promise to take good care of it. It does such a wonderful job of carrying me around, and providing me a medium for life experience.

Compared with many people I know in this University who are graduate students, I am just a little freshman. But I am determined to learn every lesson I have previously agreed to, and learn them well. *I know that I will become a graduate student and will eventually receive my Degree of High*

God Awareness. It is only a matter of time. I know this because it is what I have done in my conventional education. I will not waste time when I should be studying for repairing or fixing my body (my beloved study kit).

I will be a good student and take proper care of "myself," or my study kit.

9. I AM A MULTIPLE ENTITY IN THIS UNIVERSITY

In the previous chapter I distinguished *myself* from *my body,* which has been given to me to study my lessons in the University of Life. In this chapter, I would like to make another distinction.

Hardware and Software, or My Body and Soul

With the proliferation of microcomputers everywhere now in conventional universities, it is only appropriate that I make a comparison between them, particularly their hardware and software, and a similar system in the University of Life.

If you go to any conventional university now you will see microcomputers with somebody operating them. The uses of these computers have become so widespread that you wonder how we survived without them. I have particularly found word processing to be great fun, and even making mistakes (as often as I do) to be affordable.

It is appropriate to review the operation of microcomputers in conventional universities. I do not want to delve into the history or causes of the computer's widespread popularity. Whatever the reason, life is now difficult without them.

The Structure of Microcomputers   A microcomputer consists of hardware and software sections. The hardware is that part of the computer which is tangible and you can see — parts such as the chips or memory unit, the monitor or screen, and keyboard. Software is that which you cannot see, but without which the computer is useless. It consists of mathematical equations, words, symbols, etc., which have all been converted into special codes and stored there. The place to store all such information is generally on a "floppy disk." The disk is just a vehicle to contain all these "soft" parts of the system. It can be as floppy and thin as possible. These disks must have a certain rigidity in order to be handled with ease.

To use a microcomputer, you input the software into the hardware, letting it control the unit. At this point, whatever you input through the keyboard enters the memory and can be stored instantly on the software. The software may have unlimited capacity and store everything you input. Of course, you can write over the old information with new data, in a sense erasing the old programming.

Microcomputers in this University   Returning to the University of Life, let's examine the idea of microcomputers. I can look at myself and everyone else as one of these "microcomputers." There are currently over five billion of us on this University campus, or the world. There are two parts to these computers, too. I will call them "software" and "hardware." The part you can see, touch, and is tangible can be called "hardware," and the part you cannot see or touch (although you know it's there) is referred to as our "software".

My body is the hardware. The software is that part which represents my personality and emotions: affection, anger, fear, love, intuition, and intelligence. All other finer or "softer" parts of my life are included here as well. This is the more subjective "me," and constitutes my *soul*.

I am all these programs or feelings, written in a code and stored on something very similar to the floppy disks of conventional microcomputers. My soul or my true Self is that which is indelibly inscribed onto my life's "floppy disk."

For my software to be developed to perfection it must interact with the rest of the world. The only way to accomplish this (as with conventional microcomputers) is to use hardware. This hardware is my body.

My soul has accumulated all my feelings and emotions since the time I started to take on a material body, and combine with my hardware. My soul is my consciousness which never dies and yet continues to grow. My body, however, changes constantly, eventually wearing out, or dying. It is in the process of degeneration, while my soul is always regenerating and progressing.

Change of Hardware to Accommodate my Software In the beginning, when I was only a small consciousness, my software contained only simple programs. Therefore, simple computer hardware (or bodies) were sufficient. Because of the simplicity of the computer programs, bodies such as plants and animals were sufficient. As I grew in consciousness and more complicated programs were inscribed on me, then more sophisticated hardware became necessary. I then chose the human body as suitable hardware, and began my evolution within the Human Kingdom.

The Difference between Human and the Conventional Software

I differ from the software of the conventional microcomputers in many ways. For one thing, I choose the hardware and the people seemingly responsible for its manufacture. To work with my hardware partners for many years, I shop around to find the most suitable manufacturers. Then I place the order. This I do by first "turning on" my so-called parents. From the time they receive the order until they are ready to deliver their new hardware, nine months is generally needed. When in a rush, some can even command a faster delivery date. While my hardware is being built (and without anyone's knowledge) I sneak in and put myself into the hardware. There I recombine with it, and come out together as one package, unit, or entity.

My hardware is first very small. People, particularly the ones (seemingly) responsible for its manufacture, have fun with it. I laugh at them and have fun too. They think that is all I am — just this little "cutie hardware." They do not know that I am an old soul or software, containing so many ancient programs newly combined with this young body or hardware.

There are of course some people (although not too many as yet) who know that I am much more than this little thing they get so attached to and love. Among these, there are even some who, by looking at the hardware can tell what kind of programs are inscribed on my software!

Interacting with my Hardware While "in there" waiting for my hardware to reach a certain size to be delivered, and immediately after the delivery, I am busy learning and growing in consciousness. You see, I do not waste any time for my needed growth. Because I do not respond to adults with adult behavior, they think I do not understand anything. They think I am just a little baby or "a kid." I may be even more experienced than they are, and often, I am. In reality, my hardware and I keep changing all the time. I get overloaded with programs everyday, particularly when my body or hardware is very young looking. I continue inputting new programs (or new learning experiences) until I find that my body or hardware has become too worn out because of many years of usage and stress, and needs replacement.

Separating from my Hardware When I find that my hardware is all worn out, too old, and becomes incapable of interacting with my software, I separate myself from it, and leave it behind. To many people it is quite noticeable when I do so. Some researchers have even found out how much "I," or the software or my "floppy diskette" weigh. The weight is very small: on the order of a few grams or ounces.

It is amazing how people get so attached to their hardware or those of their relatives and friends. In some places, they even try to preserve them, as if it really mattered. This is very much like the people who save their old clothing not wanting to give it away and move on to newer, better clothing.

Overwriting Old Programs When I separate from my hardware, I have already overwritten some of my old programs with new ones. So my software during each successive recombination with a new hardware becomes slightly better than it had been.

Attaining freedom from my hardware, the software or my soul now contains a higher degree of God awareness or consciousness than it did before. I keep on attaining new hardware or bodies for myself and thus, I move up. As I do so, I keep on "overwriting" my old programs, replacing them with new or better ones.

The Objective of Combining with New Hardware

I know that with all these comings and goings, I will eventually reach a state of consciousness or awareness where I will see nothing but goodness, have only love and respect for everyone and everything, and want nothing but goodness for the whole world. It is at this level of development that I will be awarded the Degree of High God Awareness and become totally free of this sluggish human body or hardware. Now I have much more of God's powers than I ever had before, and can do more of the things God does on His higher levels. At this juncture in my spiritual development I no longer need to return to this University, or combine my software with a new hardware, unless the Master wants me to do so. I want to show my brother souls how they can advance by overwriting their old programs with new ones.

The Contents of My Software

All my thoughts, wishes, actions, efforts, emotions, feelings, etc., are included in my soul, or are recorded on my floppy disk. The accumulation of all this constitutes my transcript. I mentioned earlier (in chapter four) that it is possible for visiting professors or master teachers (who come to this University on special missions) and many psychic people, to have limited access to one's transcript.

What would happen if such transcript, or the transcript of your present academic year, became public? Imagine that this transcript, which contains everything about you in this life time, has fallen in the hands of the editor of a popular newspaper and has been published on the front page of this publication. Worse yet, imagine that the editor has devoted the entire issue of its publication to your transcript and has a lot of pictures to make it easier for the readers to learn about you. What do you think about this? Would you be fired from your job, would your parents desert you, or your spouse divorce you? Would you be kicked out of society and have no place to go, no food to eat, and no place to stay? How badly would this event effect you?

Although the University Master has maintained complete confidentiality over all His students' transcripts, what if some of the information about you (and the things I've mentioned above) would actually be revealed? What would you do?

One thing is certain. If you do not fear this event, it is unlikely that anything bad will happen to you. Our experiences are actually a matter of our attitude, and how we interpret events. We often think it would be disastrous if we lost all that we had. Most of us live in fear of losing our jobs, families, and social status. Most of us are not free, because we are emotionally attached to "ownership" of these.

Perhaps you think that publishing your life story is fine, and that God will provide everything you need. You may even be willing to give everything you have, to become more aware of God's presence in yourself. You sense how beautiful and pleasant it must be to feel such closeness and oneness. To have this bliss, giving everything we have is but a tiny sacrifice. And, it seems that when we "give up" and release everything, Life rewards us in full measure.

Several years ago I saw a movie which was about a young, athletic lady who became paralyzed in a diving accident. She was miserable with her confinement, with losing her mobility, with all the places she could no longer go, and all the competitions she could not participate in. She finally met a young man who introduced her to the Bible and the concept of God. She started feeling a oneness and closeness to God within her, and eventually became an evangelist. When a reporter asked her if she would trade her present condition with what she had before her accident, she said she never would. Of course, it is ideal to be healthy and have God too. But if she had to choose, she would not have traded what she had gained with what she had before her accident, or with anything in the world.

I have heard about many other people who lost things in their lives, but because of their faith in God, their attitude and their choices, *perceived these events in a positive way*, thus enduring them. They turned problems into solutions, illness into a medicine. This makes sense. After all, the "reality" of the outside world *depends on how we perceive it*. Looking at a flower, a bird, a bee, or a man, everyone beholding it will perceive it differently. So it is **us**, and not our external environments, which bring happiness or conflict into our lives. No one else is responsible for our joy or the lack of it in our lives. Our attitudes and belief systems make the difference, and *it is all up to us*.

10. I AM A DROPLET OF WATER IN THE OCEAN

In chapters eight and nine I distinguished myself (the soul) from my body which I called my "study kit," and my "hardware." Here in this chapter I would like to compare myself with a droplet of water, following it in its journey through life and its many experiences.

I have been wandering around the world as a droplet of water for a long time. One day, when I was just a little patch of water vapor in the air, I rose and with many of my friends, formed a cloud. It was so much fun to ride the winds and the thermal currents, utilizing what the scientists call the "buoyancy forces." I felt so good to be with so many of my friends, and to be suspended, carefree in the air.

After being totally surrounded by nitrogen, oxygen and a few other gases, this was the first time that "we," (most of the water-vapor particles in the region) were in the majority. We were actually holding our own gathering, or convention. Suspended somewhere up in the sky, away from all the troubles of the Earth, I was attending my first all-cloud convention! Everybody was giving speeches about how it is to be "down there," confined within some strange-looking objects, and not being able to move around. I had no idea what they were talking about. You see, this was the first time I was "up there" with my friends, my buddies.

Our convention was in its third day of deliberation, and we were just about to vote on an important resolution: how we could hold on together, and not have to return to Earth. We wanted to be "up here" all the time, and

69

have more freedom to move about. Suddenly a strong wind blew us apart.
It was like an earthquake. Everybody was screaming and running for cover.
When you are part of a cloud, however, you don't have too many places to
hide. I was holding on to some of my friends as tightly as I could. That did
not seem to work at all.

Then I decided to simply let go of my efforts and see what would happen.
*It felt good when I gave up trying to hold on to something, and decided
simply to ride the current.* I was then taken to a strange and cold place. I
didn't like what was happening to me, but I somehow realized that if I
stopped my resistance and just let go, I would be better off. Suddenly, with
all these changes taking place and my buddies complaining, I saw myself as
a beautiful little snowflake dancing to the ground. This was quite a new
experience. I was so much smaller now than before. Furthermore, I could
not move about as freely. I could only move down, and if the wind so
desired, she would move me here and there. Finally I arrived at the ground.
Many of my friends were already gathered there. There were so many of us,
that we were literally stacked on top of each other like blankets. Anytime a
new snowflake landed, there was a cheer for him or her, as if everybody
knew it was better to be together, rather than being alone in the world. I
was happy to be with my friends again. Here we were almost holding
another convention. But I knew that things were not the same as when we
were up there in the sky.

Here, we were assigned the job of keeping the soil under us warm. My
friends told me that this was very cold country, and if we did not do our part,
the soil and all the life therein would freeze and no vegetation would remain.
With no vegetation, then there would be no animal life, and so on. I did not
know what they were talking about. I was glad, however, that, while I had
lost all of my freedom of movement, at least I could be of some help to the
soil, and keep some poor soul (soil) warm.

My stay there did not last long. The sun started shining and the air was
getting warmer. I could see changes taking place in myself. This was akin
to a little child reaching maturity and beginning to see some changes in him
or herself. Next thing I knew I was a drop of water going down through the

soil. It was such a strange feeling to move through all those dark places. I did not like the feel of it at all. I wanted to be free and move about in the sky, not in a dark and tight place like here. I was resisting hard, but to no avail. Then the strangest thing happened. There was this octopus-looking object with a lot of hair on its legs. I did not like it a bit, but could not help being drawn to it. There was something about the whole object that forced me toward him. I was grabbed by his hairs, and in a gulp swallowed by him.

All of a sudden I was in new territory, and supported by the whole environment. Never before had I experienced being so needed and respected. Everyone in my new "home" praised me constantly, and appreciated me so much. I loved what was going on. They told me that their lives actually depended on fellows like myself visiting them once in a while. I was actually saving their lives by delivering nourishment to them. It felt so good to be wanted and needed. When I told my new hosts about all the places I had been, and that I still had a long way to go to reach my destination, they became more appreciative of my visit. They offered a little prayer for me: for God to help me reach my final destination sooner.

Although I was enjoying myself, I still did not have any idea where I was. My new friends told me that I was now living in something called grass. They identified themselves by some other names too, but frankly I did not want to know the details. I had not known that grass had different identities, nor that they took pride in these types and species. I thought such behavior was exclusive to human beings who took pride in their separateness. Anyway, being wanted was a great feeling.

I had quite an itinerary while in my new residence. Every day I visited different floors of this new home, and liked it very much. As I moved upstairs to new floors, I got the feeling that the outside world was near. Actually, I could see the light peeping through the thick windows of the house.

Early one morning, when I could see the sunlight coming through the dense windows of my house, I felt a set of sharp teeth cutting away part of the "residence." I did not have time to complain, resist, or even ask for help. The whole house, except for its foundation, was in turmoil and was being churned in a very funny place. I was being tossed around a lot. I particularly did not like being pushed around so much.

My environment now shifted, and I soon realized that I was welcome in this new place, too. My new job was to help keep a four-legged being alive. Just knowing that I was needed again was a great relief in itself. I travelled to strange places inside of this being, and participated in many activities which scientists call "processes." I also saw many funny-looking objects of all shapes and sizes. I was happily contributing to the teamwork that was necessary for keeping this creature alive and well.

The worst experience was when I entered this chamber with many of my friends and was pushed through a narrow gate into a long passage. When I asked what was happening they told me that we were being dispatched to far away places and that my job was to deliver food to many hungry cells who were working in different parts of this body. Again, I felt happy. For some strange reason I discovered that whenever I am helping someone or something, I feel good about myself.

I was quite content in this new residence. I delivered food to all those cells and on my return I carried some of their waste or garbage. So much waste is generated these days. This went on and on, and I was getting tired of it. One day something very strange but pleasant happened to me. The outside weather had become so hot, and this four-legged creature was so miserable keeping himself cool, that I decided to help the poor fellow out. In one of my rounds when I was quite near his skin, and could see the sunshine coming through his tough coat, I found a little hole there and got out. It was strange to feel the wind blowing on my face. I did not know what to make of this new experience. I wanted to go back home and continue delivering food and carrying waste. I wanted to be with my friends again. But somehow I could not return to where I was. Besides, I kind of liked it here because I felt a sense of freedom again. I became content, and knew that I could provide this poor creature thermal comfort.

I was not in this location long. A wind blew over me and cut me lose from my platform, carrying me with it again. The poor creature now really cooled off. This was a process the scientists called "evaporative cooling."

I was free at last and could move quickly over a large territory. A lot had happened since the last time I had been free. I felt I was now a pro. I had been a lot of places, and helped a lot of beings. It was a wonderful feeling to be free from all kinds of constraints.

While enjoying my freedom and dancing around in a large space, I saw some of my old cloud friends. They invited me to join them at their new all-cloud convention. There were many I had not met before.

Being the sociable cloud patch that I was, I found it easy to meet and make new friends. In fact this friendship became so strong that I was nominated by some of these newcomers for an office in their organization. I was very honored by the respect of my peers. Their respect was based on my friendliness and my seniority. They thought that I could help their convention by simply sharing my experiences with them, and telling them how best they can live their lives so that they may reach their destination sooner.

They appointed me to become a cloud-counsellor. This idea pleased me because not only had I earned the respect and praises of my peers, I also had the opportunity to help my fellow beings. This was such a great feeling: the feeling of being loved and respected.

Again, during our convention, a strong wind blew us apart, dispersing us far and wide. Cold weather settled in, and I was separated from my buddies. I was transformed into a droplet of water again, in some strange territory. This time I knew that I was there to serve plants, animals, or people, so I was not bothered. I simply decided to follow the flow.

This cycle continued for generations. After another "lifetime" as a water droplet and serving different creatures for various purposes, I finally attended what turned out to be my final all-cloud convention. While I was getting tired of changing phase (or face) so many times, I somehow knew that this convention would be my last.

Predictably, this convention was broken by the wind and I was blown away. I turned into a water droplet and landed on a river which was moving fast. I was glad I was not isolated in some confined place. I was moving fast upon a stream and saw a lot of my old friends. We were so happy to be together again. We reached a large lake and stayed there for a few days. I did not like to be stagnant again, and was afraid that I may be whisked away once more — to another cloud convention or four-legged creature. I felt that I was actually passing through a very special "leg" of my journey, and that I was in a safe place. I felt that I would not have to attend any more cloud-conventions.

I was talking to my buddies and having a good time in a relatively safe place, when suddenly I began moving very fast through a long pipe. This pipe was much wider than the passages that I have been accustomed to. I was moving much faster, too. Then I was forced to hit a large number of metal blades over and over again. It was so painful to bump into hard, lifeless objects. But, by this time I was a pro, and knew that there was a reason for all of this. *Once I let go again, deciding to offer no resistance* and to experience all this hardship, *I felt peaceful and calm.* Then, an inner voice told me that my activity was generating electricity which brought light into people's life. I was happy again to be of service. The feeling of being useful once again helped me calm down. I was able to simply enjoy whatever happened to me from that point on.

Generating electricity was by far my hardest experience. I could not have endured it (and perhaps would not have been assigned to it) if I had been just an amateur droplet. They tend to give the hardest tasks to the professionals, letting the newcomers just watch and learn. Even though generating electricity was hard, I felt calm and serene inside. I knew I was being of service.

I now completed my hardest assignment yet. I had just finished going through a hydraulic turbine and pounded on its blades. Next, I was flowing in a calm, beautiful river behind the dam. Somehow I knew that this was my *last* journey, as I was now surrounded by many loving friends. They were all like myself — just little droplets of water. There were a few whom I had not met, but that didn't bother me or anyone else. We were in total love and harmony with each other. We had become such good friends. We all knew that we were moving toward our final destination.

Ours was such a beautiful journey. There was not a speck of impurity among us. There were fishes and children swimming within us, but none of them were a bother. They could not prevent us from the last leg of our journey. I was happy that even during this juncture we provided a habitat for some creatures, and swimming enjoyment for others.

My final destination was getting closer. I now felt the anticipation of getting there and becoming one with my beloved again....

The blessed moment arrived! At last, I was one with the ocean!

It was so wonderful to feel such oneness. This was the greatest experience of my long life: to be in the ocean, merged with my beloved again.

While there, enjoying every moment of my existence, I realized that I had been one with the ocean all along. I simply had remained unaware of this. Upon consideration, I realized that I had all the properties of the ocean. In fact, I was actually manifesting the ocean in different ways! It had been so easy to remain unaware. I asked myself why it took such a long time and so many excursions for a little drop of water like me to make this breakthrough. Why did it take me so long to realize that I had always been part of this Source of Love and Life? God willing, some day I will find out. Could it be that the "Ocean" is having fun with Itself on this cosmic stage, in the play called "Life"?

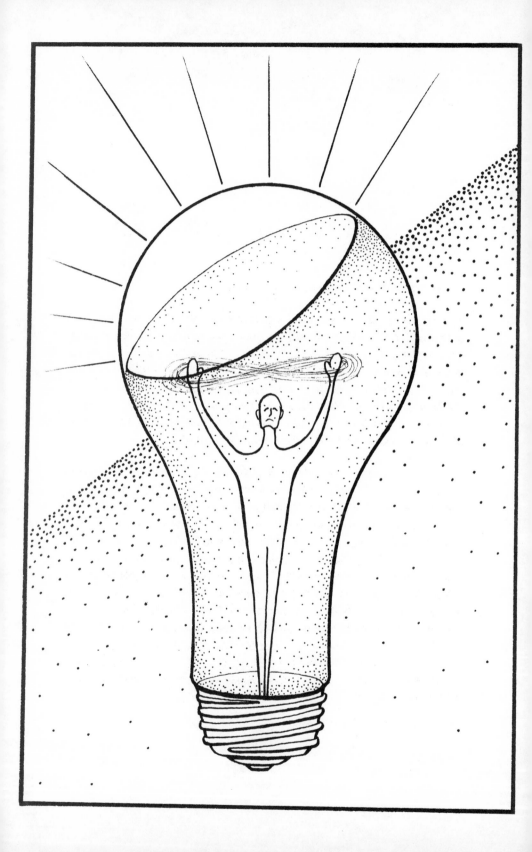

11. I HAVE ALWAYS BEEN WITH HIM

The power of God has always been with me.

Actually, I have never been separate from Him. I have only been unaware of this power and of His presence. This is like an analogy of three siblings, ages 6, 12, and 18, who have just inherited an equal amount, say one million dollars each. The older child knows he is a millionaire and can put his money to use. Because of his age, the middle one is barely aware of his fortune, and is too young to use it. The younger one, on the other hand, while still a millionaire, is totally unaware of this. He needs to grow up and reach a mature age before he can claim his fortune.

Man, as viceroy of God on Earth, has been using some of the powers delegated to him by God. Man has been using some of God's powers to create. Our world is full of man's creation. Look around and see what we have created. Look at all the things we are enjoying now which we did not have a century ago: electricity, radio, television, telephone, automobile, roads, household appliances, airplanes, spacecrafts, computers, and much more. These are all the creation of man. *He has used the power of God within him to do this,* although he may not call it such. He will still accomplish more. There is no limit to what man can do. *He has God's energy in him as human potential. All he must do is convert this potential into kinetic energy or creativity, and let God's power manifest itself into action through him. This we have been doing by coming to this University of Life and learning our lessons and becoming more aware of God's presence within us.*

77

How much of God's power I can convert to kinetic energy and manifest as action depends on how far I have come along and where I now stand in the spiritual hierarchy. Prophets and the other masters of this University have demonstrated some of God's power which we call miracles. But they have also mentioned that what they do is nothing but the will of God or the power of God manifesting itself through them in the form of miracles. They have also said that when God wills, everybody can do the same thing as they have done, and even more.

We are all like huge light bulbs already connected to an infinitely large power plant called God. The reason I do not shine and radiate this light outward is because my light bulb is covered with layers and layers of dirt. Dirt such as selfishness, ego, and separateness. I need to scrub off this dirt. I am removing it by having chosen to come to this University and learn all the hard lessons of life. The teachers who are particularly giving me hard times are the ones assisting me in removing my dirt.

Removing the dirt of ego and selfishness which has covered my light bulb requires many lessons. This takes place during many academic years. I know I will eventually rub off all of the dirt covering my light bulb. This will allow the light of God to shine through me, brightening the paths of others who are following this shared path Home.

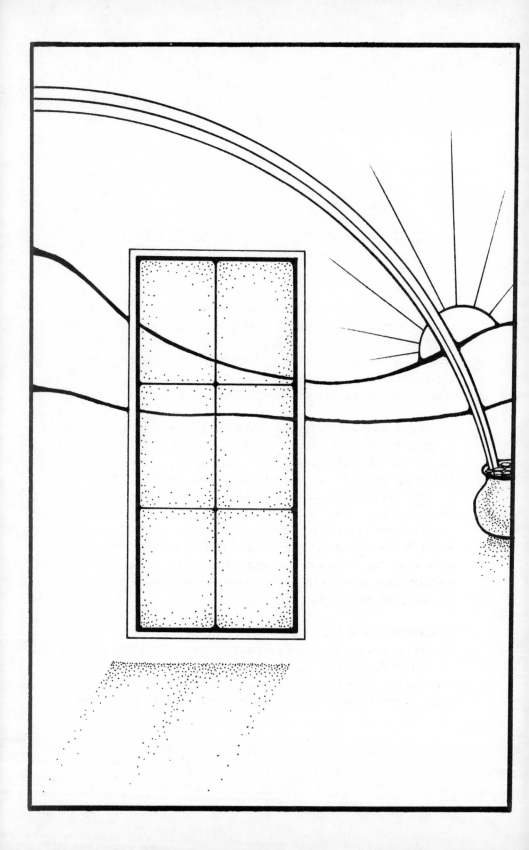

12. THE REASON FOR ESTABLISHING THE UNIVERSITY OF LIFE

This is a deep philosophical question to which I don't quite have an answer. I believe there exists only on thing in the world and it is called "God." He is the first and the last; He is what we see and what we don't see. Everybody and everything is a manifestation or a face of Him. It is impossible to "see" Him as He truly is. We only perceive Him by looking at these faces or manifestations through our limited senses or awareness.

Imagine someone asking me to draw a picture of a bird without using anything external to my body. I could probably bite my finger to let it bleed a little and then draw the picture of the bird on my chest or leg. Everything is from me, and the bird is how I have manifested myself. Now if a person looked at me whose vision was limited to the color red, he would only see the bird. If you asked him to describe me, he would probably tell you that I was just a bird. If the person's vision could be expanded, he would then be able to see more than a bird. This is similar to the popular story about three blind men who were asked to feel and then describe an elephant. Their descriptions were all different, depending upon which parts of the elephant they had touched.

Another example is to be in a building surrounded by a large and beautiful garden. Let's suppose that this building has a very narrow window in one of its walls, and that I look through it. What I would be able to see is very limited. If this garden were full of flowers and trees, arranged in groups, I could only see the ones which were in my line of sight. If roses happened to be in my line of sight, and if someone asked me about the garden, I would tell him that roses were everywhere. *To become more aware of the garden, I need to widen my present window, and even open other windows in other walls of the building.* The ideal would be, of course, to have an all-glass building, just the way the control towers in airports are, or simply tear the walls down and be entirely out of doors in the garden.

God has created us with limited senses (or windows in the building of our body). Through these, we communicate with our surroundings. For example, our eyes are sensitive only to a very narrow band (called the visible band) of the electromagnetic radiation. There are many animals which have stronger eyesight than we do. The same is true about our other senses.

In manifesting Himself as any one of the millions of species living on this planet, God chose to provide narrow, but different, "windows" (or senses) through which each entity could communicate with its surroundings, thus learning about life. To man, He not only gave the physical senses to communicate with the outside world, but in the walls of the building of his creation, He also provided a small slot so that man could gain additional awareness of the outside garden. Man could then marvel over the masterpieces of creation. God further gave man the ability to open this slot and make a window out of it — a window with no limit to its width. God gave man the ability to make this window wide enough to cover all the walls, or even break and eliminate these walls!

He made man so that he could become one with the entire Creation, or the universe. But He wanted man's awareness of his true being to grow gradually. For this purpose, He designed the University of Life and admitted all of us into it. He wanted us to gain experience and, slowly but surely, learn the lessons of life. He wanted us to drop all ideas of separateness, and to believe and feel our oneness with all Creation, our Universe. This, apparently, He did not give to the other creatures in the same degree.

God could have created us like the other creatures with a fixed level of environmental awareness. He could also have created us to possess a certain knowledge of our world, so that we would not have to go to school to acquire it. He could have created all of us to be geniuses. He could have done lots of other things. But, He chose to create us the way He did: to gradually grow in awareness of our oneness with Him. Why? I don't know. There are endless possibilities.

Perhaps He wanted to have variety in His manifestations. Why did He want to have variety, you may ask? The only answer which comes to my limited mind is that He wanted to have fun with Himself. It is all Him, anyway. The universe is just a "one-God-show."

You may now be asking why we (He) must suffer so much and experience pain through our growth and awareness process. My pain and suffering as a student in this University are due to my ignorance. I am not yet fully aware that I am a true manifestation of the Divine, and that I am representing a face of Him in the most beautiful and unique way. I am still living in that "building with no windows," kept in complete darkness, and ignorant of what is going on in the garden around me. *It is my ignorance and my lack of awareness of God within me which has made me unhappy and distressed. It is painful to be ignorant.* Once I "see the light," however, I can change!

I can't help but believe that, by designing the University of Life, and sending us (Himself) through it, He is accomplishing something important. He is making us become gradually aware of who we truly are. Perhaps He just wants to have His best faces displayed on Earth and to enjoy His own cosmic game. I believe that everything, being a manifestation of God, is only beautiful; that it is only with our limited awareness or vision we see it differently; that everything is wonderful as it is; that it is located in the right place, and it is functioning in the most perfect way. Therefore everything deserves my adoration.

The above concept is of significance in my life in that *I choose to accept things and people as they are.* Everyone is learning his or her lessons the way they have chosen to. At the same time, I do not expect anything from anyone, knowing that *everything I need is given to me by God.* I also believe that I do not need to worry about anybody or anything, because they

are all taken care of by God, and are all in good hands. **Of course, this
does not mean that I should be passive and do nothing.** Just to
the contrary! I will use all I have in my power, including (most impor-
tantly) prayer. I will ask God for guidance in discovering what is best to do
in any given circumstance. I will then do it. **The "best" always is for
the benefit of all concerned and not just myself.** With all these
practices, if what I want to accomplish does not materialize, I will accept
whatever comes, believing that it must be better for me. I realize that the
Divine Will always knows what is best.

This acceptance is similar to my going to a country restaurant, looking
at the menu to see what I like most and what "sounds" good, and then
ordering a meal. The lady who is running the restaurant and who knows the
contents of all the foods begins to serve me a different meal, saying that this
one is better for me. This proprietor, who is like a loving mother to
everyone, makes it clear to me that because of my lack of awareness and
familiarity with her foods, what I have just ordered contains a great deal of
fat and salt which are not good for my health.

Although I had taken all the necessary steps to eat (I did not stay home
saying that if God wanted me to eat, someone would knock on my door and
deliver a pizza or something else) and had used my judgement to select the
best meal I knew, I found myself being served something entirely different
from my expectations! The important thing is that I must not fight and
become miserable. Rather, I will learn to accept what has been offered me
by this loving lady, and then learn to enjoy it. This is how I adapt to God's
will.

How are the events or the decisions we choose (or "need") to make in our
lives everyday any different than the above example? In every event I must
make use of all my abilities and all that I have at my disposal, to reach the
best decisions and act upon them. If what I wanted to happen did not come
about, I would not fight the world and become miserable because of it. I
learn to accept all outcomes, believing that in the long run this would be
better for me. I can also do everything in my power to effect positive
change, both in myself, and on this planet. If I wanted change, I take

action. I am persistent and faithful. Yet, if life brings something entirely different, I learn to adapt.

In my everyday life I meditate and pray to the Master. I ask Him to show me how best I can live my life, in order to be of service to all the students in this University. I will ask God to give me the ability to trust Him and totally surrender to His wills. This way, I may accept whatever happens to me or comes my way as part of the unfolding curriculum of Life. This curriculum gives me the lessons I need to learn in order to grow in God awareness in THE UNIVERSITY OF LIFE. I pray that He may give the same to all His other students, *the one family of Humanity*.